SIXGUN CARTRIDGES & LOADS

THE END
OF A
COYOTE RACE—
KILLED WITH A
.45 COLT

A String of Jackrabbits killed by the Author in trying out some of his bullets in the .357 Magnum Revolver

SIXGUN CARTRIDGES & LOADS

BY ELMER KEITH

A manual covering the selection, use and loading of the most suitable and popular revolver cartridges

SILVER ROCK PUBLISHING

Publisher Warning: Given changes in gun technology since this work was originally published, some suggestions in the following pages may no longer be relevant or safe. This work should be treated as a historical document. The reader assumes full responsibility for any actual loading or firing of firearms.

Published in 2016 by Silver Rock Publishing

Sixgun Cartridges and Loads
ISBN: 978-1-62654-567-0 (paperback)
978-1-62654-568-7 (casebound)
978-1-62654-569-4 (spiralbound)

Cover image: Black & White Close-up of Cowboy Holding Peacemaker gun by RoGa_Pictures, Courtesy of iStock by Getty Images

Cover design by Justine McFarland
Studio Justine

CONTENTS

SIXGUN CARTRIDGES AND LOADS

FOREWORD

For the past twenty-five years I have experimented extensively with all of our available revolver and automatic pistol cartridges which are suitable for game shooting, defense or target work. Most of my early shooting was done with the old cap-and-ball Colts single action revolvers, or as we in the West are apt to term them "Sixguns." I have seldom heard a revolver called anything but a "Sixgun" or "Sixshooter" except during my two years of School of Instruction and participation in the National Matches at Camp Perry, Ohio. For this reason, I will probably term the revolver a "sixgun" more often than I will use its theoretical name throughout the following pages.

During most of my life I have had a good sixgun within easy reach at practically all times. Until 1929 I rode saddle broncs, packed, punched cows and ran trap lines most of the time; during much of this work a rifle would have been an encumbrance, so the sixgun was taken along instead. While punching cows, that sixgun usually fed my cow dog and very often myself as well. On some few occasions it undoubtedly saved my life, as well as furnished needed food for the table. Sometimes it was necessary to put a three legged horse out of misery, or to end the suffering of a hopelessly bogged cow critter. At other times, I occasionally encountered a coyote out in good open country, and when my cow horse could carry me within range of the little sage wolf, my sixgun ended his days. At other times it furnished the needed bait for lynx, bobcat and badger sets. Many times I have found little calves starved to death on the range because they had tried to sniff at a porcupine whereupon the quill pig had given them a rap across the face with his tail, filling their noses so full of the barbed quills that their mothers would not allow them to suckle and starvation followed. Several of my ponies have also had their noses filled with quills because they became too curious for their own good; so I always take time out to end any quill pig's existence with a sixgun slug.

Each year during grouse season, I killed a great many of these fine birds while hunting cattle. When a kid in Montana, I kept a record of the grouse killed with my old .32/20 S. A. Colt, which ran 42, 41 and 43 birds for the three successive years. The great horned owls were also often encountered, especially in the winter when riding along the little stream beds which were lined with leafless cottonwood and willow trees. During one single winter while at Durkee, Oregon I killed 32 of these birds with a .44 Special S. A. Colt, thereby saving the lives of a great many grouse, quail and rabbits.

I do not believe in hunting or shooting big game with a sixgun when it is possible to use the rifle; nevertheless I have often encountered big game while out riding with no rifle along, or where a rifle would have been in the way and out of the question. On these occasions I have used the sixgun, killing seven mule deer, three elk, one mountain goat and one cougar with it. My early cow-punching days showed conclusively that while a sixgun was not needed for defense very often, when such need did crop up suddenly, it was needed damn bad and the most powerful loads available were none too heavy then. Many times I have been wound up while roping off a green colt. At other times, I have been in equally bad positions by my horse sticking a foot in a badger or dog hole and turning a flip flop. On some of these occasions I have been pinned under the horse, at others I have been dragged for some distance.

Many times I have roped and dragged bogged cows out of the mud, then gotten down off my nag and "tailed 'em up," only to have the ungrateful critters ram their tongues out a foot, let out a beller and give me the race of my life if my horse was not within easy reach. Sometimes they were so

VI

weak they could make only a few short jumps and then pile up again, causing me to repeat the tailing up performance. Any old cow poke knows all about this, and the danger in it at times from half-wild range cattle. Cattle are run and worked today in much rougher country than in former years, being forced back onto the rough Forest Reserves by lack of the open ranges where they were formerly run.

My early sixgun shooting showed conclusively the need for better shaped bullets having more stopping and killing power, so early in the game I began my experimenting, trying to improve the then existing revolver cartridges by hand-loading them with various shapes or types of bullets and powder charges that were usually maximum. I occasionally tried out some weird combinations, and have had three sixguns blow up in my hand while learning what they would stand and still hang together. In all these experiments, I always tried those loads out on some sort of game or stock to find out their limitations. Finally I went so far as to design some sixgun bullets for the firm of Belding & Mull. Later I worked out some still further improvements in bullet design for the Lyman Gun Sight Corporation. These last bullets have proved so perfectly adapted to my needs that I have been unable to develop any further improvements in their design. My bullets were not the result of a little catalogue reading, but the result of many years of study and actual use on the range on game and stock. I have spent a great deal of money trying out every new gun and load that appeared over the horizon, as well as considerable time in reloading and experimenting for each sixgun or auto pistol in order to find the best cartridge.

Owing to the fact that I have written a good many magazine articles on these subjects, my mail each month contains a great many inquiries on various handgun cartridges, guns, or their reloading and shows conclusively the need for a book devoted exclusively to sixgun reloading. In the following pages I will endeavor to give an account of as much of my experiments with different handgun cartridges as possible, and what I found to be the best cartridges for different purposes. I will endeavor to cover the actual reloading of such cartridges step by step so that the beginner will have a good working knowledge to start out with. This book will be devoted to the cartridges themselves and their reloading, while the different types of guns, their sights, holsters and use will be covered to the extent of my own experience in a companion book to follow later. The subject is too big to be completely covered in any one small volume.

My own experience has shown the advisability of beginners adhering strictly to light or normal loads until they have had *plenty* of actual experience in reloading. There are so many minute details that can cause excessive pressure, and so many things that will have to be actually learned *by experience alone,* that I consider it best for all beginners to start out with moderate loads. A considerable amount of my early experimenting was done by the cut and try method. With little to guide me, it is a wonder that I did not have some serious accidents. Later, I had expert coaching and I wish to take this opportunity of thanking the following good friends who gave unselfishly of their knowledge and experience to help me: Chauncey Thomas, the late J. D. O'Meara, the late John (Packer Jack) Newman, Ashley A. Haines, S. Harold Croft, John Emmett Berns, Ed McGivern, Pink Simms and Major D. B. Wesson. I also wish to give our splendid cartridge and powder companies due credit for much valuable data that would otherwise be impossible for any individual to obtain, as well as all the firms now making reloading tools. And I better also give Mr. J. R. Mattern a vote of thanks for his most excellent book, *"Handloading Ammunition,"* from which I have derived a great deal of help.

ELMER KEITH
North Fork, Idaho
December, 1936

CHAPTER ONE

Why We Reload For Our Sixguns

Most beginners (and all should do so) in the pistol and revolver shooting game, usually start out with the little .22 Long Rifle cartridge. In this way, they can soon learn the rudiments of proper form, stance and trigger squeeze, without the effects of recoil and report of the larger calibers. This is essential if they are to become really good shots. Later, after they stay pretty well in the black of our standard revolver and pistol targets, they will want to take up the heavier calibers. Very much shooting with the latter soon runs into money, and this brings up the question of how to shoot more for less money. If they have the time available for reloading, then much experience will be gained and money saved, but if their time is really valuable, then little is to be saved over the price of factory loads.

In many cases the factory loads will not offer the required killing or stopping power, or the bullets will not be so shaped as to be suitable, even for small game shooting. Others will require very light target loads for their large caliber guns for target practice, ones having little recoil, yet cutting a large hole in the target paper, and giving every possible advantage through the scoring. Such loads are especially desirable for some forms of rapid fire work, where the recoil of heavier loads is more disturbing and it requires longer to get the gun pulled back in line for the next shot. Some will want to gain a better knowledge of their gun and loads through experimentation and rolling their own. Many peace officers and some civilians and army men will want more powerful loads than those obtainable from the factory for most calibers of revolvers, ones that will stop with certainty and with one shot any criminal or holdup that they may come in contact with in the performance of duty, or to save their own lives or their pocket books. Others, living back in the hills prospecting, packing, punching cows or surveying may wish a really powerful gun and load for emergency use on game when a rifle is not available or when the latter would add too much weight to an already overloaded back packer. For such, reloading is the answer, for in the main these cartridges are only obtainable by reloading or purchase from some custom loading outfit.

Sixgun barrels and cylinder throats are varied a great deal in diameter by some makers, even when made for the same cartridge. To get the best accuracy out of these guns which vary from the standard groove specifications, the ammunition will have to be handloaded with bullets of proper diameter to fit that individual gun. This occurs to a much greater extent than many shooters realize. Colt guns seemingly have more variation in groove diameter than do Smith & Wesson arms for any given cartridge, at least I have noticed this over a long period of years. Because the individual gun may have a bore and cylinder throat either larger or smaller than normal this does not necessarily mean that it is not fully as accurate as one having standard dimensions, but it does mean that to get the best accuracy from it, you will have to reload. I have seen factory ammunition of all makes which was loaded with bullets too large for certain guns, pressures were very high and the accuracy rotten. I have owned two .38 Colt Officers Models with groove diameters as small as .354″ and when used with standard factory ammunition they simply would not give good accuracy, yet when properly reloaded with bullets sized down to .355″ or at largest .356″ they gave splendid results. The finest S. A. Colt I have ever owned or seen will not handle some factory loads. The gun of which I speak is a

.44 Special with a groove diameter of only .4265", and when used with factory ammunition large enough to completely seal the bore of a normal .44 Special Smith & Wesson (which usually runs .430" groove diameter), the bullets are much too large for this Colt. The pressures run up as high as magnum loads, making it difficult for the gun to stay in your hat at 50 yards, yet with proper reloads with bullets mikeing as large as .428", that gun will shoot with any sixgun made, at about any range for accuracy.

Another pair of cartridges that often cause trouble with factory ammunition, are the .44-40 and the .45 Colt. Years ago a great many Single Actions were turned out in these calibers, some of the older ones, in .44-40 caliber having groove diameters as small as .423", often giving excessive pressures and poor accuracy with factory loads made for guns with a groove diameter of .427" to .429". The older .45 Colts were quite often made with groove diameters as small as .450", while the factory loads are today made for guns with a groove diameter of .454 inch. Often the cylinders of these old guns were only .450" in the throat diameter. I have yet to see accuracy obtained by swaging lead bullets ahead of 15,000 or more pounds pressure to the square inch, and for the chap who wants to get really good results from such guns, the answer is to reload. Much pleasure can be derived by any shooter in loading his own ammunition, aside from the purely cost-saving consideration. Reloading will help pass many long and otherwise quiet hours, especially during the long winter evenings, and for some will become a hobby that will last throughout their lives.

At least half the cost of factory-loaded sixgun ammunition is covered by the cartridge case itself, and in that case if fired only with non-mercuric primers it will stand reloading from ten to twenty times, depending on the power of the load used. Thus the ammunition cost is cut in half, if one's spare time is not figured in the bill (for many this spare time had much better be spent in reloading ammunition than in some other pastimes I could enumerate). After the ammunition is loaded, the desire to see how it performs will also take one into the open to try it on targets, pests, or game. Shooting is one of the finest of all sports for red blooded men and women, whether with rifle, shotgun, sixgun or the time honored long bow. The assembling of your own ammunition will give you a practical working knowledge of the weapon, and very often a confidence in it that would be otherwise unobtainable. It is a pleasure to know exactly what is in every cartridge you shoot, and what can be expected in the way of accuracy and power.

At least three-fourths of the sixgun shooters of this country are men of limited means, and, as factory ammunition soon stops the average shooter by its cost, it is only by reloading that they can ever become the good shots that they wish to be. Another great reason why we should all reload at least part of our ammunition, is that in case of war, revolver, as well as rifle ammunition, is often very hard and sometimes impossible to procure. The shooter is then out of luck unless he loads his own ammunition. Let us hope we are never again engaged in another war, but none of us can name any good reason or offer any proof that we will not be, and well remembering the time I had during the last one in getting either ammunition or loading tools that were capable of good work, I would stress the necessity of all shooters now tooling up while really good, accurate reloading tools are obtainable. In case of another war, most of our loading tool companies will then be turning out contract work for the government and will have no time whatever to cater to the needs and fancies of the average individual. It is also well to keep a stock of powder, primers and cases well ahead against the time of need when they cannot be purchased. If and when such a condition does again come about, the handloader will not be so seriously handicapped and can continue his shooting, while the man who depends altogether on factory ammunition may many times be out of luck.

Cheap practice, obtainable only through reloading will enable a great many more men to become really fine shots than would otherwise be the case. The saving and reloading of the fired cases permits saving most of the expense incurred in shooting sixgun ammunition. Today with the exception of two .38 caliber cartridges, and the .45 Colt black powder load, most revolver cartridges are under loaded, and do not bring out the full possibilities of the arm. Most of our sixgun and auto pistol cartridges are loaded with round nose bullets. These having little shocking or killing power in proportion to their caliber, generally slip through flesh with little upsettage, punching only small holes. These round point bullets also glance readily on bone and deflect from their true course. Flat point bullets do not do this. With the relatively low velocity possible in most revolver cartridges, flat or hollow point bullets are a necessity if the maximum killing and shocking power is desired.

The factory wad cutters go to the other extreme, and are very seldom accurate beyond fifty yards, because they offer too much resistance to wind and atmosphere to hold up well at longer ranges. So, with the exception of the recently developed .357 Smith & Wesson Magnum, all our real revolver cartridges must be handloaded for best results in game or defense shooting. The .32-20, .38-40 and .44-40 are not revolver cartridges at all, but rifle cartridges loaded with a rifle powder that will not burn to its best advantage in the short length of a revolver barrel. So in order to obtain best results with these particular cartridges they *must* be hand loaded. True, they are loaded with good killing, flat point bullets, but they need powders suitable for the short length of revolver barrels. Most real sixgun cranks realize this and either handload themselves or if they do not have the time, hire such work done by custom loaders. I have performed a lot of this work in the past years for men, who, knowing that the most efficient and best killing loads were only obtainable through reloading, were willing to pay any price for handloaded ammunition. Now, in partnership with W. L. Dickey, I still engage at times in this work. There is very little profit in it and I have only taken it up in order to make such loads possible for the man that has not the time to prepare them himself.

I believe the above material covers some very definite reasons why the shooter should reload. Now let us take up our pistol and revolver cartridges, and point out their good and bad points and select the best and most suitable of them for the work in hand. After this, we will take up their handloading step by step, so that the beginner will have at least a basic reference for his work.

CHAPTER TWO

Handgun Cartridges and Their Possibilities

The following list covers about all the cartridges used in revolvers and pistols in this country today, but it does not cover some obsolete cartridges as well as many foreign ones. It is not complete, but includes all the best handgun cartridges and is a thoroughly representative list.

.22 Long Rifle Rim Fire, also the Short and C. B. Caps.
.22 Winchester Special Rim Fire.
.25 Stevens Rim Fire.
.25 Colt Automatic.
.30 Luger Automatic Pistol.
.30 Mauser Automatic Pistol.
.32 Colt Automatic.
.32 Short and Long Rim Fire, now mostly obsolete.
.32 Smith & Wesson, Short and Long.
.32 Colt, Short and Long, now mostly obsolete.
.32/20 W. C. F., for S. & W. or Colt revolvers.
.380 Automatic, for Colt, Remington and other pistols.
.38 Smith & Wesson.
.38 Rim Fire, practically obsolete.
.38 Short and Long Colt.
.38 Colt Automatic and Super .38 Colt Automatic.
9 m/m Luger Automatic Pistol.
.38 S. & W. Special and .38 Colt Special.
.38/44 S. & W. Special.
.357 Magnum Smith & Wesson.
.38/40 W. C. F.
.41 Rim Fire, for Remington and other deringers.

.41 Long and Short Colt, outside lubricant.

.41 Long Colt, inside lubricant.

.44 Russian.

.44 American.

.44 Smith & Wesson Special.

.44/40 W. C. F.

.45 Colt Automatic.

.45 Auto Rim, for Colt and S. & W. revolvers (1917).

.45 Colt, for revolvers.

.455 British, Short and Long.

.50 Remington Navy Pistol.

The small .22 Rim Fire cartridges are all very fine little loads for practice shooting with both revolvers and pistols, either single shot or automatic. The **.22 Short and C. B. Caps** are also fine for short range, indoor practice where the noise of the Long Rifle cartridge is objectionable or where the backstop is not stout enough for its use. All beginners should use the .22 caliber arms for practice, and most expert shots also will do well to indulge in a great deal of this small bore pistol practice if they would remain in good shooting form and reduce the cost for themselves.

I believe it is always best to use only Kleanbore or some other form of non-corrosive, rim fire ammunition with greased lead bullets. All the copper or silver plated type of bullets without lubricant are more or less abrasive to the bore of the weapon and will give a shorter barrel life, as well as poorer accuracy, than the plain greased bullets. They also tend to cake the bore and the ends of cylinders of revolvers with a hard, dry fouling that is very hard to remove. The same applies to .22 automatic pistols. While it is true that such plated bullets can be carried loose in the pockets, they are not nearly as good as the greased variety. The recent Peters and Remington film-kote are lubricated with a hard, dry wax which is really a lubricant and while they seem to deposit more lead flakes in the rifling than plain greased bullets, they are much superior in this respect, in .22 caliber arms, to any dry, plated bullets with either nickel or copper plating.

For finest accuracy in these small bore handguns, **the .22 Long Rifle** cartridge should always be selected. The Shorts and C. B. caps, mentioned above, will do for short range indoor practice, but where match accuracy is wanted, only the various makes of fine .22 Long Rifle, greased ammunition should be used, preferably the match grade at that. Where small pests are shot with such pistols and revolvers, as well as small game like squirrels, cottontails, frogs, grouse and quail, the hi-speed, lubricated, hollow point bullet cartridges are to be preferred. They may not be necessary on such small stuff as snakes and frogs, but they certainly are with squirrels and all other small game. Our big grouse will very often get completely away, even when the hollow point hi-speed loads are used, unless he is hit exactly in the right place. Through experience I have grown to prefer larger calibered arms than any .22 rim fire for grouse shooting. Remember, that a revolver or pistol with its short barrel does not develop the velocity or killing power of the longer rifle barrels, and while these .22 rim fires can be used very successfully for small game shooting, they are not so good even for such work as larger centerfire cartridges with correctly shaped flat or hollow point bullets. I have had big fox squirrels get away, very often with a .45 auto slug through them, while shooting during a visit in Missouri on my way home from Camp Perry, Ohio. I have seen plenty of grouse get away with all manner of .22 Long Rifle bullets, often when fairly well hit, so I think it advisable to use heavier cartridges. However, for ground squirrels, pack rats, or the regular slick tailed eastern rats, the .22 L.R. hollow point cartridge is very good. This load will also afford almost unlimited practice at very small cost.

The .22 W. R. F., commonly known as the .22 Special, offers more killing power than the plain .22 Long Rifle and when loaded to the present hi-speed velocity, is a much better killer than the latter. It is not quite as accurate, having never been developed to the extent of the Long Rifle and, having the bullet seated deep in the case, is not so well adapted for really fine match accuracy. It is plenty accurate for any handgun game shooting, however, and will shoot much better than anyone, except a highly expert pistol shot can hold. I always liked this cartridge much better than the Long Rifle for game shooting. It seemed to kill better at all ranges when loaded to hi-speed with hollow point bullets.

I do not consider any .22 caliber revolver or pistol as any sort of a defense arm, with any type of ammunition, although plenty of men and women been killed with even the little .22 Short cartridge. The .22 Long Rifle and .22 W. R. F. have ample penetration to kill instantly if they strike a man's skull squarely, but unless properly placed, they are not in any sense to be depended on as manstoppers. These small bullets cause very dangerous wounds and more infection usually arises from such wounds than from those of larger caliber bullets. The bullets themselves are harder to locate without an Xray and the wounds clog up, as well as often become infected from the germs carried into the wound by the lubricant.

Almost any .22 cartridge is dangerous. A friend of mine, Mr. S. A. Camp of Ovando, Montana, showed me the skulls of four black and three grizzly bears he had trapped and killed in one season with a Colt Police Target revolver chambered for the .22 W. R. F. cartridge. Only one had to be shot a second time. Camp, with the wind in his favor, approached very close to these trapped bears and as quietly as possible, calmly waited until the bear's head was down as he bit at the trap. He would then plink them in the top of the head, so that the little bullets struck the skull squarely. They penetrated completely through! In spite of the many accounts you will hear of even heavy rifle bullets glancing off the skull of a bear, this story is true. The one that had to be shot twice was hit very close to the top of the brain pan, and although the bullet penetrated completely through the skull, it passed along the top of the brain and did not destroy the brain tissue. It put the bear down instantly, but as he was not dead, Camp gave him another one. Please understand, I do not recommend such a small gun for this work; I consider a heavily loaded .44 or .45 caliber much better for even a *trapped* bear, but have written of this merely to show what can be done by a very cool, experienced woodsman and hunter. Steve Camp does not know the meaning of the word fear, and being a taxidermist, knows exactly where the brain of a bear is located and where the skull is thinnest, therefore knowing exactly where to plant his little bullets to do the trick. Even a hog's skull will glance all rim-fire .22 caliber bullets unless struck squarely.

I once killed two mule deer with a K-22 Smith & Wesson sixgun, but consider it merely a damn-fool stunt, nothing more, and not only unsportsmanlike in the extreme, but the height of foolishness. I shot those deer in the head, and in each case, although I knocked them down with every shot, they would get up again so that I had to shoot each several times before getting one of the .22 L. R. hi-speed bullets into the brain. Later, I finished a wounded mule deer with Jim Robbin's Colt Woodsman, but I had to shoot him several times. He had already been hit twice with a .30-06 so I did not want to shoot him up any more with the rifle; however, I found out before I was through with him, that I should have given him another rifle slug through the lungs and been done with the business. This cooked any such notions I may have then had in my head of using a .22 to finish off wounded game. I am all through shooting big game with such an inadequate weapon.

I used the .25 Stevens rim fire many years ago in a Stevens single shot pistol and liked the cartridge very much indeed. It was a much better killer than any .22 rim fire that I used at that time, and is a cartridge that should prove well worth bringing up to date and improving. It would make a splendid small revolver cartridge for target practice and small game shooting; but with the .22 L. R. leaving nothing to be desired from the target shooting angle, it would be useful chiefly as a small game cartridge. However, any one having only one such small caliber revolver, could well use it for target work also, especially practice shooting.

The little .25 Colt Auto. cartridge is one I have never been able to find a legitimate use for, in either gun or cartridge. I consider it a joke. The gun is too small and short barreled for very good shooting, and the grip too small for anyone with reasonable sized hands. The cartridge is expensive and certainly is not as good a killer as the .22 Long Rifle hollow point, hi-speed cartridge. It is sold as a ladies' gun for self-defense, but I, for one, think that said ladies would be better armed with a S & W or Colt short barreled revolver chambered for the .22 L. R. cartridge, like the Colt Bankers Special. Even that is totally inadequate as a defense weapon for a woman to use and any such person is better armed with a S & W or Colt two inch barreled .38 Special revolver. With the latter loaded with any factory full power, wad cutter load, one has something that may at least discourage a holdup, and with a properly hand-loaded hollow point bullet, would be quite effective. The little S & W hammerless .32 and .38 revolvers are also much better for a defense weapon for a woman than this .25 Colt auto pistol. Such a pop gun, with neither fine accuracy or adequate stopping power to merit its sale and manufacture, will have no further space in this little book.

The .30 Luger cartridge and pistol offer the shooter a very accurate small bore, high velocity automatic. I have done and seen done some exceptionally fine game shooting with this weapon. The cartridges are expensive and it does not pay to try to reload them. Empties are thrown out into the grass and brush where it is hard to find them and new components are costly so anyone using this arm had as well stick to factory ammunition. I never liked the guns, chiefly on account of their usual creepy, hard trigger pull and the long reach to the trigger, which, with my short fingers, made a poor combination. Just the same they are, in the better quality pre-war guns, very accurate arms. I have seen several mule deer killed with them. While this gun does not offer the shock and killing power of heavier caliber cartridges, a man used to it can place his shots pretty well. It is slow to get into action as a defense weapon. The penetration is usually very good, but on the whole, I do not consider them as good a gun as the Super .38 Auto Colt. But to give the devil his dues, I honestly believe better long range, two handed shooting can be done with them than with the Super .38 Colt, especially if they are of the long barreled version of this arm.

A good many experienced woodsmen swear by the Luger and kill considerable game with it and, all told, it is a good weapon for the man who likes it. I do not. The Luger is at its best in the 9 M M, thus offering a great deal more killing power than the one of .30 caliber. Again, the 9 M M offers little shock with its metal patch bullets, and is an exceptionally accurate shooting arm with fine penetration, and, when properly placed in the heart or lung area, is a good killer. As above stated, however, it seldom offers the shock necessary to put things down and out with one shot.

My friend, Bill Bell, had an old sow bear with cubs jump on his favorite dog. Bill ran up to very close range with his long barreled 9 M M Luger and gave the sow the full magazine with the muzzle of the gun almost touching her, without putting her down. He continued shooting into her shoulders and neck to avoid hitting his dog. However, the bear tore the dog to pieces anyway. Bill said if he had had a .45 Colt or heavy loaded .44, he could have dropped that bear easily, with the same placing of shots, with one or two shots at the most. On the other hand, Jim Ross, a well known Canadian guide, swears by his short barreled 9 M M Luger. He kills moose or caribou when needed with it, with lung shots. I have seen Jim do very good shooting with it at all ranges.

The .30 **Mauser** cartridge is in about the same class as the .30 Luger, offering fine long-range accuracy, often better than many of our own automatic arms, but with relatively little shocking power. It is the ugliest, clumsiest automatic arm of any I have ever used, usually coming with a shoulder stock of wood which also forms the holster. By using both hands and the extension stock, they will shoot like a rifle, but are neither a handy arm nor one that can be brought into action quickly. The very light, small caliber, metal patch bullets offer relatively little shocking or stopping power. They are about as handy to carry as a Thompson sub-machine gun and about as much a thing of beauty.

The .32 **Auto Colt** cartridge and gun have seen long service in this country, both in the Colt and other auto pistols. It is a very good light, automatic cartridge but has very little actual killing power. In the Colt and other pistols it gives good accuracy, especially in the Colt. I have used this little gun to knock over rabbits and grouse for camp meat, and although quite accurate, owing to its short sight radius it is not so good for even this purpose as a longer barreled Smith & Wesson K-22, or Colt Woodsman, or other good .22 caliber revolvers. It is a pocket gun, pure and simple, but one that to my notion does not have nearly enough shocking power to be considered an adequate weapon for defense purposes. It is not as good an understudy arm for men who are using the .38 Super and .45 Colt Autos, as the Colt Ace .22 on the .45 frame. I believe it finds its chief sale in the cities for a small, easily concealed pocket arm; certainly it is not popular in the West.

The .32 Rimfires are now used only in some very early single action S & W revolvers, and are now obsolete for all practical purposes, so they need not be mentioned further.

The .32 S & W Long, or as it should have been named, the .32 S & W Special, is a very good little cartridge and we have some fine target arms for it in both Colt and Smith & Wesson makes. This little cartridge is superbly accurate, and will give the best of target results up to reasonable ranges. It has very little killing power in the factory load, even for grouse and rabbits and the game will have to be hit just right to be sure of clean kills. I used a Police Positive Target model Colt for this cartridge for years when a small boy and shot it often, both as a practice arm and on small game. In fact, the first sixgun I ever shot—when I was ten years old or less—was a Police Positive Colt .32 with six inch barrel and plain fixed sights. While going home from a fishing trip, we stopped at an old bridge across a small stream. A picket-pin or ground squirrel stuck his head out through a knot hole in the abutment of the bridge, across the creek some fifteen yards from us. I had shot a rifle considerably, but I had never before fired any kind of modern sixgun. A friend, who was with us and owned the gun, asked me if I could hit that squirrel. He told me to hold the tip of the front sight level with the top of the rear notch and then set the squirrel's head on top of the front sight, so resting my arms on the banister of the bridge, I did just that, and at the shot, the squirrel's head slid back slowly out of sight. When I saw the little rascal kick out below the bottom board, I was a tickled kid.

This cartridge, if properly reloaded with a good shaped, flat point bullet as Ashley Haines does, makes one of the finest little sixgun cartridges obtainable for pot shooting grouse, rabbits, squirrels and similar game. It is so accurate that a good revolver shot can place his bullet about where he wishes. Both gun and cartridges are light and easily carried, and the expense of reloading very slight, so that all in all it makes a very good small-caliber gun for anyone to practice and shoot small game with. When properly loaded with a good flat point bullet, it will kill such game cleanly; but with the factory load, it simply will not do so unless placed exactly right. The .32 Colt New Police cartridges come under the same classification.

The .32-20 is the smaller of the three rifle cartridges used in revolvers. It is a very old rifle cartridge brought out around the Seventies and was popular mainly because it could be used both in the S. A. Colt and in the '73 model Winchester as well, so that one kind of ammunition

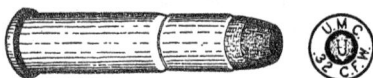

could be carried for both rifle and sixgun. The .38-40 and .44-40 became popular sixgun cartridges for the same reason. I have used the .32-20 a great deal, both in a couple S. A. Colts and also in two Military and Police models of Smith & Wesson.

The factory loads work best in the 7½″ barreled S. A. Colt, as they are all loaded with rifle powders, but properly handloaded as I used this cartridge, it is a very fine cartridge for grouse and small game. In the S. A. Colt .45 frame sixgun it can be loaded very heavily, and shot at extremely high velocity. I used the old Ideal gas check bullet #311359 a great deal with a heavy charge of duPont #80 in this cartridge, and also moderately stiff charges of Bullseye; the latter, however, not being suited to heavy loads as it is too fast and hot. This load shot exceptionally well, even to 300 yards on still days. I killed more small game with it than any other sixgun cartridge, and shot a lot of trapped coyotes, bobcats, badgers, etc. with it for years while running trap lines. I killed three mule deer with the cartridge from the S. A. Colt. However, I consider it much too light for such use.

At one time, from a seated position, using both hands and gun held between my knees, I broke a pint whiskey bottle and a quart beer bottle with this gun and load at 105 yards on a bet, before a whole double-survey crew. The first shot, being too low, I missed; however, I used it as a sighter. The next two broke a bottle each; both hit the target about in the middle. I had an interesting experience once when our crew had been back packing while running a line across some very rough country near the head of the north fork of the Blackfoot River, in Montana. It was impossible to get the pack string near part of this line, so we simply had to take our grub on our backs with a heavy coat or a lone blanket to sleep in and stay with it until through. The pack string was to be sent around to the south of us on the trail, where we were to meet it after some five days back packing. However, at the end of this time, when we hit down and cut into the trail, only elk tracks showed in the dirt. The boss and most of the crew started down the trail, thinking that the pack string must have gone by and that the elk had obliterated all traces of their whereabouts, but being used to trailing, I was satisfied that no pack outfit had been along that trail that summer, so I started back up the trail. During the last hour's work we ran onto a covey of grouse, so I killed six of them with my .32-20 S. A. Colt and placed them in my pack sack. We were completely out of grub that evening, and as I started down the trail, I noticed that Jim Flynn started following me. When I asked him why he was following, he stated that I was not going to get out of his sight as long as I had a mess of grouse in my pack. Jim and I soon located the camp, while the others straggled in much later.

The first mule deer I killed with this gun was a two year old. We were riding in an old dilapidated Ford and passed by two of them, neither of which seemed to be alarmed. I finally forced the driver to stop. Resting my hands and wrists over the back of the ancient "Tin Lizzie," I planted four 115 grain, Winchester, soft point bullets in a space I could cover with my hand on the deer's right shoulder as it staggered around in the brush after the impact of the first shot. It was very close range, between forty and sixty yards. After the fourth shot, the deer, with a broken shoulder, ran up the hill. When he stopped again, the other side of the animal was exposed. My next slug struck a limb and missed, but I planted the last one in the gun high in the spine behind the shoulder, putting the deer down for keeps. A head shot settled it.

The next one was shot at 100 yards off hand, but using both hands as only a six inch space was visible between two lodgepoles. The buck was broadside, but only the middle of the animal showed. At the shot I could plainly hear the dull plunk as the 115 grain soft point struck, then that deer and another were away in their peculiar bouncing gait. I gave that chap a couple hours, then trailed up and dressed him out. The bullet had gone completely through about the center of the body, penetrating the liver: the hole at the exit was about one inch in diameter showing clearly that it had expanded. I found several of these soft point Winchester low velocity bullets in the first deer I had killed, and all were perfectly expanded, some having the jacket completely flattened out in a sheet.

The third mule deer that I killed with this long S. A. Colt .32-20 was a very old doe and a big one, her nipper teeth being worn down almost to the gums. I was climbing a very steep mountain when someone else jumped the deer on the other side, causing them to come bounding around just above me. I saw them in time to step behind a big fir tree. A yearling was in the lead, so I allowed him to go on by. As the old doe came flashing past, I aimed just under her nose and shot; she humped up and turned down

the mountain right past me. My next shot, held in the same
way, broke her neck. At this she gave one loud bleat and
turned somersaults down the steep mountain. Examination
showed that the first soft point, 115 grain bullet struck her
in about the middle of the belly, and due to the deer being
above me and the mountain so steep, it came out high on
the left side cutting a rib in two. It had penetrated the
paunch and had torn an inch hole at the exit. The second
bullet broke the neck and also went on out through the
neck, tearing an inch hole. These three deer proved to me
that the .32-20 was too light for such shooting unless placed
exactly right.

Later I purchased a large quantity of Winchester soft
point bullets and loaded them to high velocity with duPont
#80 powder. They proved to be very much better killers
than the old, factory, low velocity loads I had used on the
deer. This high-speed hand load proved to be a much
better killer for me than any .30 Luger cartridge I had
ever used. The report was very sharp and ear splitting,
though the recoil in that heavy, long gun was a minus
quantity. I also used a great many hollow points cast in
an Ideal mould #31133. These blew up and expanded
very well indeed and were terribly destructive on such
game as chucks, jacks and porcupines, usually tearing inch
holes at exit. If cast about one to twenty they would simply
expand into a flat cake of lead. However, for most of my
shooting I used them cast about one to fifteen, in order to
hold better the rifling. Both of these S. A. Colts were very
accurate with the hand loads, but did not do so well with
some makes of factory loaded, metal patch, soft point
ammunition, the Winchester make being the only one to
give good accuracy. This cartridge, I decided gave better
killing power for me than any factory loaded .38 S & W
Special cartridge I could buy at that time, that it was far
superior to the .38 Special, if properly handloaded for these
heavy frame guns that would safely handle such powerful
charges.

Today, the .38-44 Special case can be hand loaded, with proper flat or hollow point bullets for use in .45 frame guns, to greatly exceed the killing qualities of those .32-20 loads I then used. This latter is still a very fine cartridge for revolvers if carefully reloaded, but as stated above, the factory cartridges are all loaded with rifle powder and are not so good. This small cartridge case expands very little if the cylinder is well chambered and will handle very heavy loads. With the new Hercules #2400 powder now available to hand loaders, one can load to extremely high velocity, especially if the factory soft point bullets are used, or the gas check bullets cast by hand, bought from Lyman, Belding & Mull, Guy Loverin, or other dealers such as Pacific are used.

With this new powder, velocities of these gas check bullets or the factory metal patch bullets can be raised to the same velocities as the .357 Magnum Smith & Wesson, and while they cannot quite equal the latter cartridge in killing power, owing to their smaller diameter and lighter weight, they are nevertheless a very wicked and powerful load. Although most authorities condemn this .32-20 for use in revolvers, I found it a very fine little cartridge when properly handloaded. It served me well, and altogether I still have a lot of respect for it. By shooting a great many trapped bobcats and coyotes, as well as porcupines with it, in comparison with the heavier caliber loads, as well as different loads in this .32-20, I learned exactly what to expect from it under all conditions. I consider it a very fine cartridge for the careful handloader, but if only factory ammunition is to be used, I consider it much inferior to some of the present high velocity .38 caliber cartridges. It is a hand loading proposition, pure and simple, for best results. Owing to the extreme thickness of the cylinder of the .32-20 in the S. A. Colt gun, it can now be easily and safely handloaded to at least 1500 feet with #2400 Hercules powder.

The .380 Auto pistol cartridge is a pocket gun cartridge for light, short automatic arms used for self-defense only. Many small auto pistols have been manufactured for this latter cartridge. It is superior to the .32 Auto cartridge, but is too small and light for any really serious defense work. I consider the .38 S & W cartridge very much superior to it in every way. The lead bullet of the latter offers more shocking power than does the full metal patch bullet of the .380 automatic cartridge. This .38 S & W cartridge has been used for years as a light, pocket gun load, particularly in the light lemon-squeezer Smith & Wesson hammerless, and is a very fine little cartridge in every way. It is exceptionally accurate, and if used in a longer barreled target arm, will give fine target accuracy.

I once owned a 3 inch barrel, blued finish, Smith & Wesson tip up revolver for this cartridge, with a very fine, three pound trigger pull and was often surprised at its extreme accuracy. I shot a great deal of small game with it and killed ground squirrels quite regularly up to a full sixty yards, shooting off hand, but using both hands as I usually do when shooting game. At that range it was necessary to hold up most of the front sight in the rear notch and set the squirrel on top of the front sight. It took seemingly a fraction of a second for the little bullet to get to the target, then you could plainly hear it plunk. I once competed with several National Guard officers in a match at 25 yards with this little gun against their .45 Auto Colts and 1917 Colt and S & W arms. It didn't take them long to find out that it would shoot. I have always regretted selling that little pistol, as it was one of the most accurate arms I have ever owned. For all its extremely light weight and relatively low power and velocity, it is a reliable little load. I prefer much more powerful cartridges even for self-defense, but this little cartridge has well stood the test of time, and has proved very effective for a light, short, concealable weapon in many a gun fight. The one I used so much was the hammer model.

The .38 Short and Long Colt cartridges are also very old cartridges, the Short having relatively little stopping power. It is a fine little cartridge for aerial shooting in our .38 Special arms where one wants very little recoil for fast, double action work, but even then it is much inferior for this purpose to the mid-range, wad cutter loads in the .38 Special or any number of light-bullet hand loads. The .38 Long Colt was for a time our service revolver cartridge, but proved to be totally inadequate for dependable defense use. Our troops in the Philippines found that it would not stop a man every time, even with a gun full of loads, unless the brain was struck. Several officers, after emptying their .38 Long Colts in a Moro's chest, had him keep on coming, with the result that they lost their lives from one stroke of his bolo. It is inferior to the .32-20 as factory loaded for killing or stopping, the round point bullet merely slipping through with little or no shocking power. Properly loaded with a good flat point bullet, it is a very nice load, but inferior to the .38 Special from every standpoint, as the latter cartridge will do anything the .38 Long will do and do it a great deal better, either in target or other forms of shooting.

It is not worth while to take up loading of this cartridge, as it does not offer the possibilities of either the .32-20 or the .38 Special loads. Several gun fights that have come to my notice, all prove conclusively that the .38 Long cartridge had nothing to recommend it from the standpoint of a defensive weapon, it requiring several shots to stop a man unless placed exactly right. The Philippine business ended it as a service cartridge for our troops, the .45 Automatic cartridge being adapted later. I saw several National Guard units training with it, just before they left for France in the last Great War.

My old friend Pink Simms, of Montana, was once shot through the neck in a gun fight with a .32-20 and did not know he was hit until after the row was over. This, and many other such instances, I could name, shows the lack of shocking power of most small caliber loads for defense shooting. This is not true with very powerful handloads in even the .32-20, as well as in the .38-44 case and the later and still more powerful .357 Smith & Wesson Magnum.

The old .38 Automatic Colt cartridge and its later development, the Super .38 auto cartridge are both good, accurate, reliable cartridges. The Super .38 being so much superior to the older loading, that I will only devote a small space to it. However, I did at one time own and use a .38 Military model Colt auto pistol with a six inch barrel. This gun accounted for the death of a large quantity of small game and pests. It was very accurate and flat in trajectory, making hits at long range fairly easy. With the old soft point loading the bullets expanded quite well, even tearing fairly large holes in rabbits, pheasants and grouse for me. It did not produce nearly the shock of the later Super .38 auto but seemed to do about as well as the 9 M M Luger cartridge on the game I used it on.

Later, I purchased three new Colt Super .38 autos and experimented with them on considerable game, as a comparison between that cartridge and the .45 Automatic cartridge. This Super .38 cartridge was wonderfully accurate and so flat that it was quite easy to hit relatively small objects at long range. While using these guns, I was only able to procure the Western Cartridge Co. full patch, Super .38 automatic cartridge, so did not have an opportunity to try out the Remington hollow point loads or any soft point bullets loaded to this velocity. However, the velocity of this load caused it to be a good killer on grouse, much better in fact than I was ever able to obtain with the standard .38 Special loads. Many authorities say that a soft point bullet at this velocity will not expand, but my experience has shown the opposite to be true, even in the little .32-20. If the bullet has a long, exposed, soft lead point projecting out of the jacket, it will expand with regularity on any game that offers much resistance. The old .38 automatic cartridge with soft point showed conclusively that it expanded even on chucks and jack rabbits, so I feel sure that if I could have obtained the same soft point, thin jacket bullets backed by the standard Super .38 charge of powder, that they would have produced very reliable results on game. As it was, with the full patch loads I did considerable jack rabbit and chuck shooting, and in all cases found that the much slower pumpkin from the .45 auto pistol was the better killer. The full patch Super .38 bullets would knock the chuck down, but he would soon recover from the shock and get up and go into his hole, while when hit in the same place with the larger caliber, much slower velocity .45 slug, he stayed down.

I shot them in all places, front chest shots and rear end, raking shots the length of the body, but they very often regained their feet and got away with the Super .38 full patch loads, while the .45 full patch loads generally anchored them. With the jack rabbits, which will stand considerably more punishment than most chucks, they were very often not even knocked off their feet. Even the .45 auto would not keep these tough old bunnies down unless hit just right.

An acquaintance recently wrote me about a friend of his emptying a Super .38 auto Colt, loaded with the Remington hollow point bullet, into a big cougar's chest at close range, the bullets going completely through the lung cavity from side to side without bringing him down. In fact, he had quite a time killing him as these bullets all failed to expand. I have not used them personally as they were not for sale around here at the time I was experimenting with that cartridge. However, I am sure if this cartridge were loaded with a soft point, thin jacket bullet, it would expand. Jack rabbits offer about as good a comparative test for killing power of a sixgun or auto pistol load as anything I know of, as they will stand more punishment at times than a deer, and much more than most men can ever stand. It seems they are shock proof for their size.

In the .38 Special we have one of the finest of small caliber cartridges for reloading purposes. A wonderfully accurate cartridge, that will shoot with any gun for accuracy, and one that in the heavy .38-44 cases can be reloaded with proper shaped flat point or hollow point bullets at very high velocity to give exceptionally good killing and stopping power for the size of the cartridge. Of course, such high velocity, heavy loads are only possible in heavy, .45 frame guns. With the standard loading of the .38 Special, it is a very poor killer on anything. It

has good penetration, but the pointed, round nose bullet simply slips through with little actual shocking power. I have used it a lot and have owned a great many guns in this caliber, both Smith & Wesson and Colt.

Several gun fights with this gun that have come to my notice have proved that the standard 158 grain round nose bullet would not stop a man with any certainty whatever, even with well-placed chest shots. I well remember one case that happened in Helena, where a cop friend of mine was called on to arrest a holdup in a noodle parlor. The holdup was using a short, nickel plated, break top .32 caliber revolver. He was a shell-shocked victim of the late War, and no doubt was not in his right mind. He emptied his .32 at the cop, while the latter planted all five of the loads he habitually carried in his .38 Special S & W in the holdup's chest without even staggering him. One of the holdup's bullets went through a booth and into a boy's leg who was peacefully engaged in the eating of his bowl of noodles; another penetrated the cop's breast pocket and a note book and lodged in the pocket over the heart. The holdup died on the way to the hospital.

Having shot a great deal of small game with this same standard .38 Special, I know that it lacks killing power, even for grouse, when loaded with that standard bullet. The big blue grouse will very often fly off with one of these bullets through their bodies. Even when fairly well placed, one has to hit them just right to kill with any certainty. On grouse it did not prove nearly as reliable as the .32-20 for me. Properly loaded with a flat point bullet, it is an excellent grouse gun. I once saw Herb Bradley shoot a chuck through the neck at close range with his Officer's Colt and standard Western .38 Special ammunition. The chuck was in its hole with just his head and shoulder showing. At the shot, the chuck went down out of sight. Herb said he knew he did not miss. Soon the chuck came back out and stood for another shot in the same position. We could plainly see the blood running out of the side of his neck where Herb's first bullet had slipped through. He was a dumb chuck, for Herb shot him through the brain next time.

I have many times seen jack rabbits take two or three of these loads through the lungs without moving, then jump and run off, often for a considerable distance before they start going in a circle, finally winding up in a small dust cloud as they kick their last after falling over.

The Super Police 200 grain .38 Special loads seemed to kill a good deal better on such game than did the standard bullets, even though at comparatively low velocity they had more of a wallop, due largely to their blunt points.

When the first **.38-44 Specials** came out, due to the efforts of Major Wesson and the Remington Arms Co., I gave them a thorough tryout on grouse and chucks, as well as jacks and porcupines. They killed grouse very well indeed, showing clearly the increase in killing power over the standard .38 Special, due to increased velocity alone, as they were loaded with the same round nose semi-pointed bullet. I tried them in both the plain, soft lead and in the hard point, metal tipped bullets and what little difference existed, was almost negligible, probably a point or two in favor of the plain lead bullet. Both drilled clean little holes, with little or no expansion and but little shock. When I handloaded my flat point bullet to the same velocity, it killed any such game very reliably, and when I used my hollow point bullet at the same velocity, it killed such game still better and was simply ruinous to grouse, as it blew them all to pieces.

These loads were a great improvement over the standard .38 Special, but would have been a great deal better killers on anything if they had only adopted my bullet and loaded it to same velocity. However, more about this bullet will come later. It will suffice to say that the .38 Special is one of our finest medium size sixgun cartridges and one that can be reloaded to give very fine results.

After Major Wesson had instigated the .38-44 Special, I had my friend, the late Capt. Frank Frisbie, who obtained the first mould from Lyman Gun Sight Corp. for the Keith hollow point 160 grain .38 Special bullet, cast and send one hundred of them to Major Wesson. Remington loaded them for him in the .38-44 Special case to 1100 feet velocity. These loads clearly showed the Major the possibilities of this bullet when loaded to high velocity, and formed the basis of the experiments that led up to his having the Winchester Repeating Arms Company bring out the .357 Magnum S & W cartridge with a modification of my bullet—one better suited to loading in the long .357 Magnum case. The .357 case was made longer to make it impossible for anyone to load it into a standard .38 Special gun (this would probably blow it up unless it was one of the heavy .45 frame guns). Just after the advent of the .38-44 Special cartridge, I did a great deal of experimenting with what powders were then available and my 160 grain hollow point .38 Special bullet. I found that #80 was the best powder available here at that time, so I shot a good many hundred loads with ten grains of this powder in a pair of Smith & Wesson heavy frame .38-44 and Outdoorsman revolvers. I even went so far as to load this bullet in the Remington .38-44 case with 11 grains of #80 powder. This load, with a round nose bullet, is listed in Mattern's book. I knew of several Officer's Model Colts that it had wrecked, although these heavy .45 frame S & W guns handled it perfectly, as well as a couple S. A. Colts. I wanted to know the pressure, so I sent samples to Peters Cartridge Co. for testing. They gave an average of 42,000 pounds pressure. No wonder they blew up the .41 frame Officer's Colts!

At that time I wrote Major Wesson several lengthy letters about these experiments and how well his guns handled the extreme loads. This, I believe from his letters, determined him to bring out a real killing .38 caliber cartridge and with a properly shaped bullet for game and police use. This extremely heavy .38 load with my hollow points gave better killing power than anything I had then tried in this caliber, blowing grouse up completely and killing porcupines, chucks and jacks cleanly with a shot in the paunch. When Winchester developed the cartridge, Major Wesson wished the case crimped over the front band of the square shouldered bullet to prevent marring and deformation of this sharp shoulder. This was just the opposite of my ideas when I first worked out the design of this bullet in 1929, as I wanted that forward

band to be left out of the case to help true up the cartridge
in the cylinder throat and to cut down as much as possible
the length of the jump from the cylinder into the barrel
throat. However, with the long Magnum case a re-
designing of my bullet was necessary, as when crimped in
the beveled crimping groove in the Magnum, it gave the
cartridge too great an over-all length for the cylinders of
the heavy frame S & W guns. So the point was shortened
somewhat, still retaining my shape of flat point and sharp

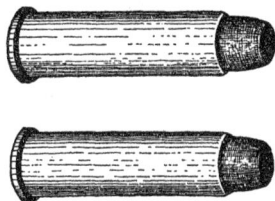

Two .357 Magnum cartridges loaded with different bullets. Upper is
the standard Winchester loading with standard factory bullet as designed
by them. Lower shows same case loaded with the 150 grain Keith hollow-
base bullet No. 358431, but seated with all bands in case and crimped
over the front band.

shoulder, but with three narrow lubrication grooves instead of one large lubricant groove and one crimping
groove as I had originally designed it. My design was
worked out for the .38 Special case. The .357 Magnum
bullet is almost a duplicate of F. C. Ness's .45 Colt Bond
bullet.

When the new .357 cartridge and gun came out, I
gave both a very thorough tryout on chucks, jacks and
other pests, and found that it had more actual knockdown
killing power on all game that I shot with it than any
other factory loaded, real revolver cartridge on the market.
It stopped any and all such game instantly—with one shot.
I also tried the gun with my hollow point bullet loaded in
.38-44 Remington cases ahead of 13.5 grains of Hercules
#2400, and found for such game it was an ever better
and more destructive killer than the Magnum factory

load. Where extreme and deep penetration was needed, the factory load, or my hollow base bullet of same design, would probably prove best; but where only some eight to ten inches penetration were needed, with as much expansion and tissue destruction as possible, then my hollow points did the work. Later I reloaded the fired Magnum .357 cases, using this same hollow point 160 grain Keith bullet with up to and including 15 grains of #2400 powder, getting even greater destruction on the pests that I shot with it. This .357 S & W Magnum load proved to have much more actual shock effect and killing power on all game I shot with it than any factory loaded revolver or auto pistol cartridge, including the .44 Special and .45 Colt. I did not test it against the .44-40 rifle cartridge from a sixgun, but I believe it would kill even better than that excellent load unless the .44-40 were handloaded with a similar powder and soft point bullets. In making this comparison, however, I am speaking only of factory loaded cartridges.

I consider the .357 Magnum cartridge a very reliable load for any serious self-defense work, Police or Peace Officers' use. I honestly believe it will stop any criminal instantly with any reasonably well placed hit anywhere be-

tween the top of the head and the pelvic bone. Even a leg or arm shot by this cartridge is very apt to put a criminal out of commission or at least take some of the fight out of him. The factory loaded, flat point, lead bullets always expand reliably and tear good sized holes through flesh, clearly showing the effect of a properly designed sixgun bullet when fired at very high velocity. Major Wesson's game shooting in Wyoming last fall further proved the worth of this cartridge, and showed that

when properly placed it would kill big game in a very
short time. I do not believe in actually hunting big game
with a sixgun when a rifle is available, or for the promis-
cuous shooting of such game with a sixgun by any except
expert revolver marksmen, men who can reliably place their
shots and who have sense enough to refrain from shooting
unless a chance of so placing their shots with certainty is
offered. However, to many, this gun and load will prove
a great boon, as at times it is impossible to have a rifle
along.

The .38-40, like the .32-20 and .44-40, are all rifle
cartridges brought out for the '73 Winchester. Revolvers
were later chambered for these cartridges to allow the
same ammunition to be used in both rifle and sixgun. This
is, to my notion, the poorest of the three cartridges, this
opinion having been formed after several years of continuous use of the caliber. Properly handloaded, it is a
very accurate cartridge and very powerful as well, but nearly all sixguns I have seen made for it were not properly
chambered. It is a short bottle neck cartridge, with a body
about the same size as the .44-40 and .45 Colt and all the
sixguns I have owned for this load had the body of the
chamber reamed about one-fourth inch too deep (or too
far forward) and when fired, the cases naturally expanded
to fill the chamber, leaving a neck on them not more than
an eighth of an inch in length, which necessitated the full
length resizing of the case each time before it could be
reloaded.

It is of course, like the other two, a black powder case
and is the hardest of the three to reload correctly with
smokeless powder. The bullet must have an adequate
crimp groove and be seated friction tight as well, to prevent its receding in the case. This continuous working of
the brass, in renecking after each shot, soon ruins the
cases; they become brittle and crack or split at the neck
or shoulder much more quickly than do straight revolver
cases that are full length resized an equal number of times.

I played with this cartridge for a long time. The flat point bullet offered good killing power, but on account of the poor chambering in every gun I have been able to obtain, as well as the renecking of the case necessary after each firing, I quit it cold. I used several different weight bullets in it, including the .40-60-210 grain rifle bullet sized to correct diameter, backed with a heavy charge of #80 duPont powder. Later, I also sized down the .40-82-260 grain rifle bullets and used them with the same powder. I obtained very fine accuracy and good killing power, but not the equal in killing power I later obtained with the .44-40, .44 Special and .45 Colt. I doubt if it was as effective as the present .357 S & W Magnum.

I experimented with about all loads the gun would stand. Owing to the walls of the cylinder, especially over the powder charge, being just about as thin as those of the .44-40 and .45 Colt and the fact that the cases expanded badly with the least over charge of powder, its pressures had to be kept down religiously or the empty cases were very hard to extract, even in the S. A. Colt gun. About as good results as any I obtained were with the factory soft point, metal patch bullet and #80 powder. This load shot very accurately and cleanly and had it not been for that cussed case expansion at the neck, I might have stayed with the cartridge longer in my search for the ideal big revolver load.

I killed considerable game with the .38/40, but I shall always remember especially one mixup I had with a big

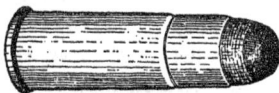

bull elk that nearly cost my life, and certainly would have but for that sixgun. It was all my fault—a damn-fool kid trick. I shot an enormous bull elk in the side of the neck at 70 yards with the Springfield and 220 grain bullet;

dropping him at the shot. He slid and rolled down the mountain into a depression left by the uprooting of a big spruce tree. When I went up to him, his head was doubled back under his brisket. Since there were two feet of snow, I could not see his eyes, and, kid like, I supposed him to be as dead as a mackerel. At that time I was sold on neck shots for big game, but this experience and some others soured me on them for good and all times.

My 220 grain bullet had missed the vertebrae and had merely stunned the old boy, lodging under the skin on the off side of the neck, perfectly expanded. I went around to the head end of him and decided, before trying to get a look at his ivory tusks, I had better make sure he was dead, so standing directly in front of him I prodded the top of his withers with the muzzle of the Springfield. I obtained instant action, for he became alive and up on his feet all in one motion. His brow points caught me in the stomach as he raised and straightened out his head and neck, throwing me down the mountain, over his back I think, but I went so fast I hardly knew just how he did throw me. At any rate, I lost track of the Springfield and landed with my hips bedded through the hard crusted snow and with my feet pointing up the mountain on top of the crust. My left arm and shoulder had struck a partly covered log and knocked me dizzy. The old bull had his hair all turned the wrong way and was buck-jumping up and down in that depression where he had slid, with his feet all bunched up, like a sheep or deer killing a rattle-snake. He seemed to think I was under him in the snow from the way he acted, or else he was still dizzy from the shock of the rifle bullet.

At any rate, I was packing this same S. A. Colt .38-40 in a belt holster, which had slipped up under my arms. I had the cylinder loaded alternately with Remington soft point, low velocity and heavy, black powder, hard bullet handloads. The Remington factory loads were some of the first brought out with the tinned or white primer. I managed to get out the gun, and as I cocked it, the bull stopped and looked at me; I think he saw me then for the first time. I planted the first shot squarely over the brain pan in the center of his forehead—a Remington soft point—and he merely shook his head and came for me. As he landed from the first jump I shot at his forehead again, this time with a heavy, black powder, hand load. He went down instantly, and slid up against me with his head again doubled back under his fore quarters.

In all my life in the hills, I have never known any man to pull off so many fool stunts as I did then with that elk, so maybe this will be a lesson to others. I got up, found my Springfield sticking muzzle down in the snow and finally managed to get all the snow out of the bore and action, but the one sensible thing I did do was to reload the six-gun and run the tie-strap around my leg and buckle it. Then I again decided to see if the elk was really dead or not, so I walked around behind him in the deep snow. His rump was up above the level of my feet on the snow crust, so, turning the safety over on the Springfield, I decided to kick him on the rump and shoot him again if he moved. At my kick he lashed out with those hind legs, knocking me down the hill again before I could even pull the trigger. Again I lost my grip on the rifle, but jerking out the sixgun I started to work on him. As he knocked me down, he jumped to his feet and started off around the mountain, running away from me. I started shooting before I quit rolling, the first shot hitting the back of the high sword prong on the left horn and penetrated half way through as I later found out—another Remington soft point. The next two shots landed one in each ham and the fourth (a heavy hand load) broke his back just in front of the hips, letting him down behind. Then the old boy pawed himself around facing me and started slowly toward where I lay on my back in the snow, pulling himself along by his fore feet alone, with his hind legs laying out behind him. His head was held high and he grated his teeth as he worked toward me. I waited until he was close and shot him squarely in the front of the neck, breaking it this time.

I have never seen a madder or more determined bull than this old boy was as he pawed himself toward me. Have never been able to figure out some of his actions, especially his running off after knocking me down the second time, but I now believe that he did not even see me after I went down. I was only a 20 year old kid then and was too tickled about getting my first really fine elk head, to use what little brains I possessed. I had killed elk before, including another six point bull, but none the equal of this one. On skinning out of the head, I found the second sixgun slug, a hand load, had penetrated back into the jaws, but had hit too low, almost between the eyes and below the brain, while the first one, a factory load, had merely splattered out to the size of a nickel on the front of the skull, without even denting it. Chauncey Thomas wrote me soon after, that some of the same caliber and make of ammunition that he tried, probably some of the same lot, would not even shoot through an inch board if solidly backed up at 50 yards. It was no wonder they failed to kill that bull. However, it certainly expanded, even at that low velocity.

I had very good accuracy with the .38-40 hand loads, even up to 300 yards, and managed to hit a running coyote through the shoulders at around this distance on one occasion, with fourth or fifth shot if I remember correctly. The purp got away, but a neighbor found him later with one shoulder broken. I liked the flat trajectory of these loads, but finally decided I needed a heavier bullet and at least a straighter case.

The .41 rim fire is a very old one and has been used for years as a deringer cartridge. At best, it is a close

range load, suitable only for very short ranges where the
smallest possible gun is wanted. I would prefer it to any
.25 Colt auto for such purpose. It is at its best in the
Remington double deringer, which gives two shots. The
caliber is good, but the bullet so sharp pointed and powder
charge so small that it is not any too effective. It is not as
good a defense weapon as a lemon squeezer Smith &
Wesson, but for the person who absolutely must have a
vest pocket pistol, it will at least discourage a holdup. If
the cartridge were loaded with about twice the powder
charge of all the loads I have ever obtained, it would be
much more effective. A gambler here once had a duel in
the main street of Salmon City with another man. He
made a poor choice of weapons, as he tried to buck a good
sixgun with a pair of .41 deringers and was quickly killed.
Colt at one time made some four and five shot revolvers
for this cartridge, called house pistols.

In the old .41 Long and Short Colt centerfire cartridge we have another very old load, probably first used in
the rod ejector, double action, solid frame Colts. This
cartridge was at its best in the old outside lubricated cartridge and when thus loaded with black powder, is still a
good defense load, and one that I would prefer to any
standard .38 Special for close range work. Later, it was
brought out in smokeless loads with an inside lubricated,
sub-caliber, hollow base bullet, depending on the expansion
of the hollow base for accuracy. This, at best, is a very
poor system and has never been very popular. If this cartridge were revamped and brought up to date using the .41
Long case with either the blunt nose or a better flat point,
square shoulder, 200 grain bullet of full groove diameter,
it would make a wonderfully fine cartridge and a darn sight
better police load than any standard .38 Special. Very
good velocity could be obtained in the thick, heavy cylindered .45 frame guns, and even in the Officer's model and
similar weight guns the velocity could be run up to 900
feet. Such a flat point or blunt point 200 grain slug would

have a great deal more slap and knockdown than any round pointed, standard .38 Special, yet the difference in recoil would be negligible. Some friends of mine have experimented along these lines by rechambering the .41 S. A. Colt to use a longer, straight shell, made by cutting off the .351 Winchester automatic rifle case and using such a bullet at very good velocity. This proved to be a fine killer. It is a wonder some company has not long ago seen the possibilities of this caliber and brought out a real cartridge, instead of letting it slide into the list of obsolete cartridges.

The **.44 Russian** is a very fine target cartridge, but neither it nor **the .44 American** which is now about obsolete, needs to be discussed here, as the .44 Special will do all that either of these shorter cartridges will do and a great deal more either on the target or for more serious sixgun work. I consider **the .44 Special** our finest large caliber revolver cartridge by a wide margin. It will do all that any .45 Colt or .44-40 will do and more. Any weight bullet that works well in either the .44-40 or the .45 Colt will do good work in the .44 S & W Special. The .44 Special will also give higher velocities with any weight bullet from 200 grain up to 250 grain or even 280 grain than will the thin-walled-cylinder guns chambered for either the .44-40 or the .45 Colt. The case, being straight, will withstand complete resizing and reloading a great many times. It is fully as accurate as anything ever produced for use in a sixgun, not excepting the .38 S & W Special and is a great deal easier to hand load for fine accuracy than some .38 Special guns. Some may wonder at this statement, but they will find the reason if they load the two cartridges for different guns of each caliber, especially if there is any variation in groove diameter from the standard. A variation of .001″ is not so much in a .44 Special, but makes quite a difference at times in a .38 Special.

In 1927 I abandoned the .45 Colt for my own use in

favor of the .44 Special, and have seen no reason to change back. I soon found that I could load much more powerful cartridges for the .44 Special than for any other revolver. These powerful hand loads extracted easily and shot more accurately than any .45 Colt I have ever owned or used. The factory .44 Special load is little more than a squib, with a velocity of 800 feet or less and owing to the shape of its round-nose pointed bullet, gives very little killing power. I have shot sage hens with Western factory .44 Specials and wounded them through the bodies, and then have them run off and hide themselves in the brush. Yet if you hand load this cartridge with a properly shaped bullet of 230 to 250 grains weight then it is a killer, and if a hollow point bullet is used, the same sage hens can be scattered all over the ground and torn up too much for table use. The 230 grain bullet can be loaded safely to 1200 feet and in long barrel guns possibly up to nearly 1300 feet with Hercules #2400 powder. The 250 grain bullet can be given a velocity of around 1100 feet with the same powder.

I once designed a 260 grain bullet for Belding & Mull, using their blunt nose shape and Croft and I also worked out a similar shape for the same firm weighing 280 grains, both for the .44 Special. These bullets were very good killers and quite accurate at reasonable ranges but did not do so well or tear as large holes as those I later designed for Lyman Gun Sight Corporation. Last year, I did considerable experimenting on chucks, jacks and other pests with the .44 Special, handloaded with my 235 grain hollow point bullet and 18.5 grains of #2400 Hercules to see if it was as good or a better killer than the .357 Smith & Wesson Magnum. In all cases it proved to be a much more powerful load and gave nearly twice the amount of destruction as the .357 Magnum, even when the latter was loaded with a 160 grain Keith hollow point bullet at standard velocity for this cartridge. Jack rabbits shot in the chest had their whole hind part or rear half blown away. On rump shots the front end of the Johnnie was completely torn to ribbons. I have never before seen such destruction of tissue from any sixgun or automatic pistol cartridge and really believe it is the most powerful handgun load in existence. I went up as high as 20 grains of #2400, but the cases showed some signs of pressure, not

The .44 S & W Special cartridge, loaded with the 235 grain, hollow-point, Keith bullet No. 429421.

nearly as much, however, as I had found with the #80 loads I had used for years. I found the limiting factor to be leading, the 20 grain load leading the guns badly with the bullet temper I was then using. A different alloy or grease wads might have stopped this, but at the time, I cut the charge to 18.5 grains, causing the leading to almost be eliminated. The pressure signs on both case and primer seemed less, even with 20 grains of #2400, than with the same bullet and 13 grains of duPont #80 powder. The velocities were much higher, as was clearly shown by the expansion and killing power. The recoil was heavy, although not unpleasant in a Colt Single Action or in the Smith & Wesson with the new S & W Magna grips, but after some fifty rounds was very unpleasant in the S & W gun with the standard style of grips.

I have handloaded a great many heavy .44 Special loads for friends who have killed elk, bear, moose and mule deer here, and one sportsman took some to Africa and kept twelve men supplied with antelope meat with my 250 grain handloads in a S & W .44 Special military model with 6½″ barrel.

The consensus of opinion among the most experienced sixgun shots of this country indicates that the .38 and .44 Special cartridges are the best of all from any standpoint, for the handloader particularly. These two are made in greater quantity than any other revolver cartridges; hence, more experimenting has been done with them than with other loads, and they are held to closer tolerances in loading. The guns chambered for these two loads are also held to closer tolerances as to groove diameter and chambering than most other sixgun calibers. To get the best out of them, they have to be handloaded, as all standard factory loads for both are very light and offer a high trajectory curve with very little actual stopping and killing power. Nevertheless, they are accurate in the extreme.

The .44-40 rifle cartridge when used in revolvers, is a good killer, in spite of the fact that the rifle powder is not suitable for short barreled revolvers. However, when properly handloaded with a pistol powder, or with heavy loads Hercules #2400, and the factory soft point bullet or the cast hollow point, it is a much better load. It is much more accurate than many would have us believe, as the results obtained with it in fifty yard test groups by my friend Ashley Haines proves that point beyond the shadow of a doubt. Haines obtained a great many groups from .44-40 caliber single action Colts running from 1½ to 4 inches at this range with his carefully assembled hand loads with #80 powder.

Until the advent of Hercules #2400, duPont #80 was the best powder for the .44-40 Colt and Smith & Wesson revolvers. This case also needed to be resized full length

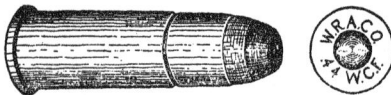

before reloading for proper results in all the guns of this caliber that I have owned. The powder chamber of this cartridge is practically the same size as the .45 Colt, and therefore the cylinder wall is just about as thin. The thinnest place occurs under the bolt stops, and excessive pressure soon bulges out these bolt stop cuts, leaving dents

in the cylinder. This, in turn, leaves a depression for the
case to expand into and makes extraction hard. I do not
consider the .44-40 nearly as good a cartridge for revolvers
as the .44 Special, which will do anything that the .44-40
will do and more. The .44-40 can be given about 1200
feet safely with the 200 grain bullet. This flat point
bullet is a good killer, but the cartridge case is not nearly
so good for really maximum loads as the smaller diameter,
straight .44 Special. The .44-40 case is so big that for all
really heavy loads either #80 or #2400 are the best
powders. The #80 is very sensitive and increases pressures, due to drying out of moisture content when stored
for any length of time. This is not nearly as good a
powder as Hercules #2400 for any big revolver case in
really worth while, powerful, hand loads.

The .45 Automatic, as far as actual stopping and killing power are concerned has proved to be the most effective
of all auto pistol loads I have used. It is a low velocity
cartridge, the trajectory being so very high that it is difficult to hit with it at long range, yet it is as accurate as any
cartridge I have ever used, especially the National Match
1925, .45 Auto pistol ammunition. I shot a great many
of these loads in a remodeled and properly sighted 1917
Smith & Wesson and did some very good shooting with
them. I killed jack rabbits and one blue crane up to a full
300 yards with this gun and load, before witnesses, but
usually I managed to hit only after several ranging shots to
find out how much to hold over. In the .45 automatic Colt,
this cartridge is a mighty effective military one for comparatively short range work where speed of fire and ease
of reloading the gun is of prime importance.

This load killed all game better for me than any of the
lighter calibered automatics, in spite of their much higher
velocities. I believe though, if the Super .38 auto had used
long-exposed, soft point bullets, it might have done better.
I only tested it on game with full patch, finding it was

much inferior to the .45 Auto in stopping power. I have had this load often fail to stop jack rabbits with lung shots, and have also had sage hens go some distance with it through their bodies. Owing to the hard metal patch and the round nose of the bullet, it does not tear flesh as lead flat point bullets do.

One time while gathering cattle with my brother, I had this S & W 1917 with me and .45 Auto ammunition. I rode on ahead of the little bunch of cattle we had gathered that day, to try to kill a couple of grouse for supper. Soon, I spotted a big cock sage hen sitting on a boulder about fifty yards up the mountain. Slipping off my nag, I used both hands and planted a metal patch slug right in the V of his wishbone, cutting off the bottom part of the heart. He fell off the rock, but caught himself and sailed over me some twenty feet high on set wings. As he went over, I hit him again, but the shot was too far back, knocking loose one leg. He sailed on down the gulch and suddenly dropped in the dusty trail right in front of my brother's cow pony, kicking up quite a dust which started the horse to pitching, but we had our supper assured anyway. The second shot had penetrated the entrails too far back to kill.

I also used a .45 Auto Colt on the trap line a great deal, both for killing trapped bobcats and coyotes, and for shooting bait as well. It killed much better than the .32-20 and standard .38 Specials, but not so well as the .38-40, .44-40 and .45 Colt with factory loads. I have known several men to be shot through the lungs or abdomen with this cartridge who are well and strong today. One friend, who was shot through the right lung, served on the Montana National Guard rifle team with me in 1924. He was a fine scout and a good shot. Early each morning he had to get out in the open and take several long breaths of air to get that flat lung inflated. Owing to its smooth metal jacket, this bullet is not the killer that the lead bullet of the same size and velocity is, but for the man who likes an automatic, it is undoubtedly the best cartridge of them all for serious work. The Super .38 will make hitting at long range much easier, but it does not seem as effective as the .45 slug when it does land. If loaded with a thin jacket soft point it might be superior. I honestly don't know about this, but I do know that in full patch bullets, my .45 was by all odds the best killer.

The .45 Auto Rim is a cartridge brought out especially for the 1917 Colt and Smith & Wesson guns, and is a very fine one for reasonably close range work. It does not have the volume nor powder capacity necessary for long range shooting that the .44 Special has, but it can be given very good velocity with several different bullets, up to and including 1000 feet. Any bullet for the .45 Colt revolver cartridge can be sized down to properly fit and be used in this cartridge. I also designed a flat point, sharp shoulder bullet for this cartridge, both in hollow point of 235 grain and 240 grain in solid. Hercules Unique is a very fine powder for heavy loads in this case. Again, the cylinder is too thin to withstand the pressures one can use in the .44 Special.

This .45 Auto Rim is one of the best cartridges of all for normal loads with some of our pistol powders like the duPont #5 and Bullseye, as it has a small powder space. I loaded it for some time with #80 with very good re- sults. When loaded with my flat point, sharp shoulder bullets to 1000 feet, it is a very fine killer and makes an excellent police officer's gun. The cylinder can be carried full of the Auto Rim cartridges, and a couple of the 1917 clips can be carried filled with rimless automatic cartridges, all which give the officer the quickest reload of any revolver.

While we are discussing this cartridge, it might be well to mention the fact that the cases as made by different factories vary greatly, some having solid heads, while others have greater powder capacity with protruding "semi-

balloon" primer pockets. These various cases require different powder charges. The solid heads, with only a
hole through from the primer, usually giving maximum
safe pressure with a grain or two more powder than the
cases with thinner heads and protruding primer pockets.
I tried to work out a load for this cartridge with Hercules
#2400 powder and my 235 grain hollow point bullet,
but had no luck. The cartridge seemingly developed maximum pressure without burning the powder properly and,
on account of excessive pressure, I was unable to reach the
stage where this powder would burn cleanly. #80 worked
well, as does Hercules Unique for heavy loads, while any
of our true pistol powders give fine results. I consider
Unique the best powder for heavy loads in the .45 Auto-
Rim, as it is a comparatively hot, quick powder, yet giving
good velocity with low pressures suitable for the thin walls
of the gun cylinder.

The old .45 Colt Peacemaker cartridge has had
probably as much use as any other revolver cartridge,
especially in the West. Up to the advent of the .357
Magnum Smith & Wesson, I considered this cartridge,
loaded with 40 grains of black powder by Remington, as
being the most powerful and most killing factory load
obtainable in revolvers. The bullet, however, is much too
pointed for best results, as it slips through game or man
too easily. In the case of man, the shock is usually enough
to put him off his feet, but not always, as I have heard
of one case where two cowpunchers emptied their .45
Colts with black powder loads into each other at a few
paces and one lived afterwards. Properly handloaded, with
a flat point bullet, this load is a very good killer. After
having trouble with the elk mentioned in the .38-40 discussion, I switched to the .45 Colt and used this load
exclusively for a number of years, killing much game with
it. It was always very reliable for penetration, but the
pointed, factory bullets slipped through too easily to suit
me.

As an illustration of this, I will cover an experience I once had in killing a mountain goat with a .45 Colt S. A. with 5½″ barrel and Remington factory, black powder loads. I ran onto this Billy just below the top of a long ridge, extending for some three miles to a very high, sheer cliff. I got in the first shot at 40 yards as he was running from me, and struck him in the seat of the pants (or would have, had he worn pants), the bullet going almost the

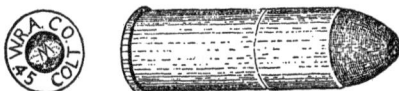

length of his body, breaking the left shoulder and lodging under the skin in front of that shoulder. The next shot hit a granite boulder that was between me and the running goat. The granite dust and particles of lead from this shot turned him up the mountain, when my third shot caught him squarely through both lungs. He then turned down the mountain, while I ran to the top of the ridge to keep above him. The country had all been burned over and was covered deep with ashes, so that it was easy to see where each shot hit. When he came out in a little basin about 300 yards below me, I again started shooting from a seated position with my back against a stump, using both hands on the gun which I held between my knees. By holding up about all of the front sight in the rear notch, I finally got the range and knocked him down twice out of the six succeeding shots. I followed along the ridge, keeping above the goat for two or three miles, shooting when I got a good chance to use a back rest and both hands, as the running at the high elevation had started my heart to pounding. I finally came up within thirty yards of the old boy and shot him broadside through the heart. This knocked him down, but he was up and going again instantly, so I shot him through the neck. Again, he went down, and again he was up and going in a second. In all,

I fired eighteen shots at that Billy goat and hit him with ten of them. He finally lay down behind a burned snag, and as I had but six cartridges left, I finished him with a blow from my belt axe on the back of the coco.

All those slugs but one had penetrated completely through the goat, punching very small holes—even the two that struck him in the ribs at 300 yards had gone right on through him. A goat is about the most shock proof creature I have yet come in contact with. Three shots had penetrated through the heart. How any animal can stand such punishment is beyond me. Anyway, I then decided that I needed a flat point bullet that would offer more shock, so I started using the 300 grain .45-90 Winchester slug sized to .454″ ahead of 35 grains of F. F. G. black powder. This load was very accurate and would stay in a foot circle at 100 yards. The pressures, however, were really too heavy for the thin cylinder walls of the gun.

I also killed a very fine buck mule deer with this gun with a shot through the neck from behind, and another big buck with a shot through the lungs as he ran by me broadside at about 100 yards. Finally, having the head of a case blow off, also blowing the loading gate off the gun and cutting a deep gash in my trigger finger, I decided I had better lighten the bullet, which I did by cutting off the rear band and one grease groove. This now made a very good bullet for the Old Peacemaker. I used it for some time, but finally, deciding I wanted to use smokeless powder, I designed a 260 grain bullet for Belding & Mull using their standard, very blunt, round nose. F. C. Ness worked with me on this and added a small band in front of the crimping groove. This bullet proved to be a very good stopper at reasonable range, but I was never able to get as fine accuracy at long range as from the revamped Winchester .45-90 mould.

One summer while riding and looking after a bunch of cattle in Southern Idaho, I stayed with a neighbor the night of the 3rd of July. The next morning being the Fourth, my friend rose at daylight and started shooting his sixgun out of the back door. I was sleeping in the attic, and not to be outdone stepped out on the little porch and started the old Single Action working. I got off the first shot alright, but at the second, I noticed that the recoil and report were particularly heavy. Shooting fast, I thumbed the hammer as the gun turned up in recoil and the third shot snapped. Instantly I looked to see if the bullet had stuck in the barrel from a bum primer—at the same time I heard something clattering around in the bed room and noticed an oblong hole through the door to my left. The top strap of the gun was gone, as was also half of the cylinder. The first empty case was alright, laying there with half its body in sight in the chamber, the second case was ruptured full length, as was the third. Both the second and third cartridges had gone off at one and the same time, why, I still do not know, but there being only one hole for them to go through something had to give way. It did—the gun was a wreck. The primer of the third case showed plainly where I had snapped on it, and also showed clearly that it had already been fired. I had fired those cases and reloaded them so many times that the primer pockets were worn or expanded oversize. I believe that the sharp recoil of the second shot threw the third cartridge back against the recoil shield hard enough to ignite its protruding primer. I can account for it in no other way. We found the piece of cylinder under the bed, that had cut through the door into my bedroom, and next day found the other section of the cylinder out in the horse corral; the top strap, we never located. I gave the frame to the late J. D. O'Meara, who made and welded on another top strap and with the addition of a new cylinder, put the old gun back in commission again.

The barrels of these guns, especially the early ones and

some later built guns, differ a great deal in groove diameter, as do the mouths of the chambers. The older ones with the screw cylinder-pin fastening often had a groove diameter of only .450″ (I have two such guns on hand right now), while the later guns had groove diameters from .453″ to .456″. The cylinder throats varied just as much. This will give anyone an idea why it pays to reload for this particular cartridge. At one time, Remington turned out some very short-case, squib loads of about five grains of Bullseye. They were not very accurate and certainly had no power, and why they were ever placed on the market is a mystery to me. I have many times sent the old Ideal 255 grain pointed bullet through eight by eight soft pine timbers and sometimes through the much harder yellow pine timber, with 40 grains of black powder, while these little Remington squibs would seldom penetrate over four inches.

The greatest handicap to the proper appreciation of or satisfaction derived from the .45 Colt is due to the fact that there are many thousands of these S. A. guns floating about that have been assembled from odd parts, with absolutely no regard paid to whether these parts fitted or not. For almost a generation, 1873 to 1894, the old Single Action .45 Colt was the service arm of the U. S. Army—I believe the artillery was armed with the 7½″ and the cavalry with the 5½″ length of barrel. About 1894, the Army very unwisely changed over to the .38 Colt double action and used this until 1911, when the present .45 Automatic was adopted. At any rate, all these old .45 Single Actions went into storage, many of them being partially scrapped or junked, until about the time of the last War when they were gathered together again and sold throughout the country for about $5.00 each. Some of them were almost worth that price. I suppose I have examined hundreds of them and all were assembled from different parts— the stock straps of one number, frame of another, cylinder of a third and the barrel from somewhere else. No proper tests were ever made after assembly as far as I can find out, but the gun was sold "as is." Most of them were a sorry bit of junk, and if you have such a sixgun, don't attempt to use anything in it but factory or normal loads.

These old relic .45's are also the reason why there is such an apology of a rim on all our present .45 Colt cartridges. Designing the cylinder of these old Frontiers was evidently the start of the Colt economy program (which they have certainly adhered to ever since), and they made it as small as humanly possible and yet allow cartridges to enter and seat. As extraction was by means of the finger rod, no real rim to the case was necessary, so today, our ammunition manufacturers have to keep supplying the .45 Colt cartridge with that joke of a rim on it.

An accident that befell a couple of friends of mine in Cleveland, Ohio, well illustrates the lack of tearing qualities of the pointed, factory .45 Colt bullet. It was well for both that they were not using flat point or hollow point bullets. One friend started to practice quick draw work with his Single Action Colt without a holster, placing the gun in his right, front pants pocket. On grabbing and cocking the gun as he drew it, the front sight caught on the front edge of his pants pocket, rolling the grip forward out of his hand, his trigger finger firing the gun at the same time. The 250 grain, pointed, factory slug struck him just over the right hip bone, slipping completely through his body from front to back, then struck the other lad in the arm, penetrating the arm and elbow and lodging under the skin. They managed to climb fences and make it to the hospital alone, as there was no one with them at the time; but they both had quite a spell of it and certainly were lucky to recover which they both did.

This cartridge is at its best when properly handloaded with my 250 grain, solid, flat point or 235 grain hollow point bullet ahead of 22 grains of Hercules #2400 powder. It then developes its maximum killing power and is very accurate. However, it must be loaded with bullets sized just right for the individual gun, and not more than .001″ or .002″ over groove diameter, *and the cylinder throats must be large enough to allow the bullets to pass through easily by hand.* Many old timers swear by this cartridge so loaded. Personally, I prefer the .44 Special, as I can send the same weight bullets as fast or faster and with fully as good or better accuracy, and have a much larger margin of safety with its thicker cylinder

The .45 Colt (long case) loaded with the 250 grain, solid, Keith bullet No. 454424.

walls. I used #80 for a time and finally ruined a good .45 S. A. by cracking the rear end of the barrel with a load of 16.3 grains #80 and the Belding & Mull bullet #454260. I then quit #80 in the .45 Colt and went back to 42 grains of F. F. G. black powder. In its place, I took up the .44 Special and dropped the .45 Colt.

With the **.455 British** cartridge, we have the largest calibered revolver load used in this country today to my knowledge. It is a great favorite in Canada, having been for a long time the British service load. This cartridge is quite an accurate one with its big heavy 290 grain hollow-base bullet. It has for a long time proved to be a fine man stopper, even though it has comparatively low velocity and a round point bullet. Properly handloaded with the Ideal #457196 with a good charge of duPont #5 or #6, **it is** a very fine cartridge for reasonable range with good pene-tration. My friend, P. M. Chiswell, has, for a long time used this cartridge in a triple lock S & W. He found this gun especially effective in the late war with Germany. Any-one having such a gun can well afford to load it with the long .455 Colt case and the above bullet, and will have fine results if the work is properly done. It is not such a good long range cartridge as the .44 Special as the cylinder walls are too thin to stand any overload.

I once used a British-made automatic revolver for this cartridge, but had only the short cartridges at the time. These were certainly squibs, and had to be placed just right to kill blue grouse with one shot. This was a Webley-Fosbury revolver and the ugliest brute of a sixgun that has ever come to my notice. The cylinder and barrel came back to the rear at each shot, operating a sort of ratchet that turned the cylinder. At another time my friend, Harold Croft, sent me a Webley & Scott Bulldog revolver to try out. This was also a good shooting accurate arm, but certainly no thing of beauty. In fact, these British made revolvers are about the homeliest and clumsiest guns I have ever used. This .455 cartridge is at its best in good Colt or Smith & Wesson revolvers. Anyone will do well to stick to them in using it.

The old .50 Remington Navy Cartridge has long been obsolete. At one time I experimented with it by making my cases from .50-70 rifle cartridges and using cast bullets. It would handle very heavy loads of black powder, but was such a huge, clumsy arm that I soon disposed of it. These pistols can be remodelled and rebarreled with hand made barrels for the .38 and .44 Special cartridges. They then make fine single shot target pistols.

* * *

This covers all the more important of our revolver and pistol cartridges. Now let us pick out the better cartridges and select the ones that are best adapted to our needs and the ones which can be reloaded to the greatest advantage. If a light cartridge is wanted for practice and small game shooting, then one can do very well with either the .32 S & W Long or the .32-20 cartridge. If for only normal or slightly heavier loads up to 1000 feet velocity, or possibly 1100 feet at the most, the .32 S & W Long will do nicely. This cartridge, when loaded with a flat point bullet of around 100 grains, will do good work with a normal charge of duPont #5 or #6, or Bullseye. The guns can be had in light weight in both the S & W and Colt target models.

If any heavy loads are contemplated, it is advisable to take the .32-20 cartridge and obtain a gun on a .45 frame with its thick heavy cylinder walls. The Colt S. A. will do nicely, and if the Smith & Wesson Company can be induced to chamber their heavy .45 frame revolvers for this cartridge, it will handle them just as well in that D. A. Smith & Wesson. Both companies make guns for this caliber in a light frame suitable for normal loads, but the big frame is advisable if very heavy loads are to be used. Always remember that the .38 Special offers a much wider range of loads and bullets, and more power.

I consider the .38 Special or its later cousin, the .357 Magnum, the finest of all small caliber revolvers. Almost any conceivable load can be worked out in these cartridges. The .38-44 Special case is the best for handloading, as it will handle a much wider range of bullets than will the .357 Magnum case, which must be loaded with the bullets seated deeply in the case, with most available designs at

.38 S & W case, loaded with the 160 grain Keith hollow-point bullet No. 358429. Normal seating for this bullet—with entire front band ahead of crimp, so it will assist in centering cartridge in the chamber. Same bullet may be used in the .357 Magnum when seated deeper and crimped over front band.

present. The .38 Special case can be loaded for light, short range target shooting, or normal loads for any target work, and heavy loads for long range, or very heavy magnum loads with hollow point bullets for game or defense shooting. With the latter two types of loads, however, only the heavy .45 frame guns should be used, as such loads require that thickness of cylinder to safely withstand the enormous pressures developed. This caliber is well adapted to most target work and small game shooting, and in the .357 Magnum, it is a fine load for game or defense work. The Magnum load is too heavy for most men for straight target work, being much more powerful than is necessary.

Turning to the large calibers for outdoor use under all conditions, and all phases of defense and game shooting as well as target work, there is nothing quite so good as the .44 Special *properly handloaded*. This cartridge is fully as accurate, if not more so, than anything so far produced and will perform with any .38 Special on the target range. Owing to its slightly greater recoil, it will not be quite as suitable for rapid fire work as the .38 Special, except when loaded very light; it is, on the other hand, much more suitable for long range and defense or game shooting, except small game. It can be handloaded to give more power than any other revolver cartridge.

The .45 Auto Rim cartridge is another very good, big cartridge, especially for the officer, on account of its very rapid reloading with two clips of three cartridges each in the 1917 Colt and Smith & Wesson arms. This one feature, as well as its low cost in some instances, is all that can be said in favor of it over the .44 Special. In all other respects, the .44 Special greatly excels it both in power and range, as well as accuracy. This is due to flatter trajectory at longer ranges.

I think that the .44 Special is to be chosen over the .44-40 or .45 Colt if the cartridges are to be handloaded. If factory ammunition is to be used exclusively then either the .44-40 or the .45 Colt offer more killing and shocking power than does the factory loaded .44 Special. In this connection, I would prefer the .357 S & W Magnum personally, it has seemed to me to be a better killer than the .45 Colt factory black powder load. While I have not had a chance to compare it against the .44-40, and can only judge by my former experience with that caliber, it seems to kill game better and more reliably than does the .44-40. Certainly, it is a much better long range load, has more sectional density and is fully as accurate as hand loads in the .44-40.

I think anyone will do well to select either one of the previously mentioned .32 calibers for a small caliber gun, or for average work take the .38 caliber, and for a heavy gun for serious outdoor use, the .44 Special. Certainly the .38 Special and Magnum and the .44 Special are our best cartridges for the handloader, yet anyone owning a gun of another caliber can produce good hand loads for it and have a good gun also.

*   *   *

I have not mentioned the reloading of the automatic cartridges, mostly because it is seldom done to advantage. These guns throw the empties out where it is often hard to find them, especially if shooting from a boat or in timber and brush. Also for certain functioning of the arms under all conditions, nothing has been found that would give such reliable results as the factory metal patch bullets. Little saving in cost is to be had by buying the factory components and loading them yourself. In the case of the Super .38 Auto, I believe more killing power could be had by buying soft point bullets and loading in new cases to standard Super .38 Auto velocities. Reloading automatic cartridges, especially the .45 Auto, has produced many troubles. The discussion as to their causes has brought about no improvement in the effectiveness of the ammunition, but has often times produced broken or badly battered slides. I think the user of the auto pistol will do best to stick to factory loads, and if he uses a Super .38 or .45 Auto Colt, he should get an Ace .22 L. R. Colt for an understudy of the larger arm and to keep his hand in. He can in this way obtain plenty of practice with a minimum of cost. All automatics are entirely and solely dependent on their ammunition for perfect functioning. If they are reloaded, then one should either load factory bullets or select bullets with a round nose and cast them very hard, about one to ten tin and lead, and stick to standard velocities.

The recoil springs of these automatic arms are regulated for one cartridge at a certain velocity, any variation from this standard is apt to cause jams and frequently some part of the arm will be broken. I am not alone in the above belief, for most custom loaders fight shy of reloads for the automatic. Most automatics are chambered rather loosely, this being necessary to insure perfect feeding and function-ing, so their fired cases will have to be full length resized. Occasionally, the cases will stretch in resizing and this again causes trouble in their reloading and often in the function-ing of the arm with such loads. Whether you only intend to shoot the neighbor's cat off the back fence, or go in for serious self-defense work, you want the arm to function perfectly and surely. By my own limited experience, I have found that this is best accomplished in the automatic with factory cartridges, no matter what make or caliber the arm is.

CHAPTER THREE

Selection of Bullets

Now let us take up the actual work of reloading our sixgun cartridge. First, we may as well select the shape, weight and design of the bullet needed for our purpose or which best suits our individual fancy. If it is for short range target practice and a light load needed, as well as a light powder charge wanted on account of absence of recoil and light report, then the shooter may as well select a bullet of normal weight, or somewhat lighter than normal if it be equally accurate. Bullets with a square front-band or shoulder should *always* be selected for serious target work as they cut clean holes which aid in the scoring, as well as often giving the shooter the benefit of the full caliber of his gun on a close shot. The true wad cutters, with an absolutely square face, are seldom accurate beyond close range and I do not favor their use as much as the bullet having a longer point.

All revolver bullets should have an adequate crimp groove for properly crimping the bullet in the case, not only to hold it against the shock of recoil, but also to assist in perfect powder combustion. A great many revolver bullets listed by our different mould makers do not have such a crimp groove and must be seated friction tight, using a very light powder charge, or else crimped over the shoulder of the front-band. I think it well to avoid such bullets. Select those having a deep, bevelled crimp groove that will aid in forcing the front edge of the case into an adequate, sure crimp. Nothing is more exasperating or better conducive to the creation of a cloud of blue-smoke "cussin" than to have a sixgun bullet jump its crimp from the recoil of the gun and project out past the front end of the cylinder, thus tying up the arm completely for the time being. Such things can be very dangerous if the gun be used for protection and they will hopelessly spoil a rapid-fire string at the target.

Modern smokeless powders require a heavy, uniform crimp to hold the bullet against the initial ignition of the charge, in order to insure its proper ignition and combustion. Some powders, such as Bullseye, are easily ignited and are not so sensitive to crimp resistance, while others, such as #80 and #2400, require the maximum in heavy crimp to burn at all, let alone burning completely or as they should for normal results. As the flash from the primer spits into the powder, it starts the ignition of the charge, building up some gas pressure at the same time. If the crimp is weak or uneven, this initial ignition may alone be sufficient to shove the bullet out of the case before all the powder is properly ignited, thus causing squibs, hang-fires or similar troubles. Often such squibs are blamed on the primer, whereas the real cause is a crimp insufficient to properly hold the bullet in the case against this initial pressure until that powder charge has been properly ignited. As the bullet moves into the barrel from such a poorly ignited charge, the pressure becomes less and less, often dropping to a point too low to even burn up the powder.

With black powder we have no such trouble, it ignites very easily and thoroughly, "exploding" at once and burning completely if loaded in the proper charge. Many smokeless powders are not only hard to ignite, but harder still to "keep going" properly and such brands require heavy crimps, and often heavy bullets as well, in order to set up sufficient resistance at the initial stage of ignition to insure uniform and complete combustion. Unless the crimp be heavy and the brass case firm and sound, that crimp cannot hold long enough for such powder to be uniformly or properly ignited. Unless so ignited, that charge cannot burn completely, and it may not burn at all but may merely drive the bullet up in the bore of the gun or just barely out of the barrel, leaving the bore and often part of the action covered with unburned powder grains.

I like a wide, bevelled crimp groove and do not care for these narrow, cannelure type of lines which some bullets carry on their front band. A bevel, slanting towards the base, is necessary for best results. To get power out of any sixgun load, it must have a strong and heavy crimp, as I have explained above, and this crimp can best be formed by considerable restriction of as much of the edge of the case as possible; the wider the groove and its bevel, the more brass we are able to "crimp" into it. When the cartridge is fired, this crimp must be forced open, that part of the front band in back of the crimp must do this forcing— and it has a lot of work to do in opening out the crimp completely and evenly. A bevel here is of considerable help in opening the crimp to the full diameter of the case mouth and thus not tear off the rear edge of the front band or the edges of the rear band which follows, possibly reducing its diameter and causing gas cutting. Experience has proven to me that small, narrow grease grooves (generally with no crimp groove) with correspondingly narrow bands are not nearly so well suited to properly forcing the crimp of a heavy sixgun case, without in turn deforming the base and other bands on the bullet. All of which is an illustration for the need of bands as wide and as strong as you can possibly get on your bullet. You need adequate lubrication, of course, but you do not need bullets so short and decorated with such a multitude of grooves that they are hard to cast, offering little resistance to gas cutting and also giving mighty little bearing surface for the lands of the gun to work on and spin the bullet in its passage through the bore.

For illustration, take the old .38 Special Ideal bullet #358311. This bullet has a perfect crimp groove, as well as a good lubrication groove, with wide, heavy bands. It is not a killer in any sense of the word, but is superbly

accurate, and where maximum penetration is wanted from
cast bullets in .38 caliber this bullet, cast very hard and
used with a good dose of Hercules #2400 in heavy frame
guns, will surely deliver the goods. All round nose bullets
tend to glance more on bone, if not struck squarely, than
do flat point ones. Most of the light weight bullets do not
have good crimp grooves, but must be crimped over their
front shoulder. With some very fast burning, easily ignited
powder like Bullseye, they give good results for close range
shooting. But for any serious target work at 50 yards, or
for hunting or defense work, where good stiff charges are
used, the bullet should by all means have a good crimp
groove and be tightly crimped in the case. No front band,
whose forward edge must be crimped over with the mouth
of a strong brass case, can be perfectly square after forcing
out that crimp and thus cannot be in best condition to perform its wad cutting or full diameter hole punching prop-
erties.

I have had Remington, .45 Colt, black powder loads jump
their crimp and tie up the gun on many occasions, and have
had considerable trouble from this source with some of my
own reloads in the .38/40. Many times I have had bullets
recede into the case where the shell was not full-length
resized. A sufficient crimp groove is also a necessity in
keeping the bullets from being shoved back into the case
when pushing the cartridges out from belt loops. This is
another reason why the handloader should select only bullets
which have a good deep, adequately bevelled, crimping
groove. All Keith bullets have properly designed crimp
grooves for the above reasons. In utilizing them, be sure
that your crimp is uniform, strong and heavy.

The base band to your bullet had also better be a wide
and strong one. I have had much trouble with narrow
banded bullets gas-cutting through their base band from a
fast or hot burning powder. Also, lubricant easily leaks
past a narrow base band and if loaded cartridges are stored
away during a hot spell it may get into the powder charge,

where it does no good. I want a wide, full diameter base band to my bullet, which will help eliminate both fusion from the hot gasses and the hazard of a squib load from lubricant leaking into the powder charge.

Another reason I prefer all the width possible to both base and forward bands on my bullets, particularly in .38 and .44 calibers, is to eliminate the squirting of lubricant past the bands and the consequent messing up of the entire bullet while lubricating and sizing it. Most of these small band, multiple groove bullets are extremely hard to lubricate without grease squeezing past their sides and getting all over both base and point of the bullet. I have found that a single, wide and deep lubricating groove will come the nearest to eliminating these faults, yet still carry sufficient lubricant for the purpose intended. Furthermore, some of the shallow grooved bullets cannot be sized down more than a thousandth or so, whereas with a deep grooved bullet you can take off a few thousandths and at times thus use the bullet in guns of different bore dimensions. In designing my .45 Auto and .45 Colt bullets, I could not get their bands as wide as I wished, due to the over-all length of the bullet being limited by its maximum weight specifications; still, they seem to work out all right but I do not like them as well as the wider bands permissible on my .38 and .44 Special designs.

Many years ago I began to look about for the ideal shape of sixgun bullet to suit my own ideas and needs. I was in search of a bullet that would not jump its crimp from recoil and which would also give the revolver its maximum killing power. With all this in mind, I first designed the Belding & Mull #454260 bullet, which proved a very good missile for the .45 Colt. My objection to this design was that I could not get as good long range accuracy with it as I wished. Later, I worked out a similar design in .44 Special, of 260 grains weight. Harold Croft and I together then worked out still another variation of this .44 bullet which weighed 280 grains, and retained the Belding & Mull blunt, round nose. On all three we had a good crimp groove and also one large, deep lubrication groove. Croft paid for the cherries for these last two bullets. We used these for some time, but the crimping grooves proved hardly deep enough. By that time I believed that I could greatly improve on their design, both in accuracy and killing power, so I worked out the first of my bullets for the Lyman Gun Sight Corporation.

I wanted this new bullet to seat out of the case as far as the length of the cylinder would permit, the same as I had done with the Belding & Mull bullets, but I also wanted a wide, heavy band in front of the crimp groove to help true-up the cartridge in the cylinder and so keep the bullet in perfect alignment with the bore while firing. This band would also act as a wad cutter for target and game shooting, rather I wanted the front band of my bullet to finish the work of its flat point and to cut full wad cutter holes in anything it struck, and with its square shoulder it does just that. At the same time, I wanted a long, flat-pointed bullet which would be better balanced for long range accuracy, yet give maximum killing power and cut full sized holes in anything it struck. At that time (1928) Harold Croft was visiting me and we spent a month, all told, experimenting with the .44 Specials. He did not think much of my design then, as he watched me make a rough sketch of it. The Lyman folks decided the bullet had good possibilities, and their Mr. Pickering had the steel model turned out and sent me for examination. This first Lyman-Keith bullet was in 250 grain weight and is listed in the catalog as #429421.

Tests with #421 on jack rabbits and similar game soon showed that it was the best killer we had so far tried; that it would not jump its crimp, and was the most destructive bullet we had then used on game. Next, I had Lyman make up another bullet exactly like it, but with a hollow base to weigh but 230 grains. Mr. Pickering again worked out this model for the new bullet from my own crude drawings. This lighter weight permitted the use of still heavier charges of #80 powder and, owing to its higher velocity and flatter trajectory, proved an even better bullet for long-range game shooting. It is catalogued as #429422 in the Lyman Hand Book. Later, when these bullets had proved to be exactly what I wanted, I sent Lyman similar

Keith 230 grain, .44 Special, Ideal No. 429422

designs for the .45 Auto Rim and .45 Colt, both in solid, flat-base type to weigh 240 and 250 grains—#452423 and #454424 respectively. The illustrations of these bullets in the #31 Ideal Hand Book are transposed.

These two .45 bullets proved to be so very good in their respective calibers that I determined to finish the job and design a similar bullet in .38 Special. I had first worked out the design of this bullet in 1929, but did not send it to

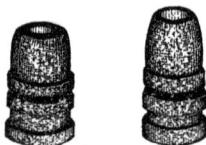

Left sketch is the .45 Colt, Keith hollow-point bullet No. 454424, weighing 235 grains. Right is .44 Special, Keith hollow-point No. 429421, weight 235 grains.

Lyman until some years later. This bullet weighed 173 grains in solid form, but was too heavy to group-in with the sighting of several guns which I tried it in,—usually shooting so high it was necessary to add height to the front sight or cut down the rear sight. It shot to about right elevation with the S & W heavy duty .45 frame gun,

but altogether too high in my Outdoorsman. Then, for me,
it did not seem to shoot very accurately with light charges
of powder, at least not in my guns. But Don Martin used
it exclusively and still swears by it in his target S & W,
Military and Police Model.

I asked Lyman to make up another bullet exactly the
same but with a hollow base to weigh 160 grains—which
they did. My friend, Charles B. Keller, was working on a
similar design, but when he saw this one, he said it was
exactly what he wanted and was about the same thing as
his design. This bullet proved to be very accurate, a good
killer, and entirely satisfactory in every way.

When I first worked out this design of sixgun bullets, I
believed that the flat point, combined with the groove
diameter front-band, would give killing power enough for
any purpose, but I wrote Lyman that if anyone wanted even

Keith hollow-base .38 Special, 160 grain bullet, Ideal No. 358431

more shock they could get it by adding a hollow point to
the flat-base models. The late Capt. Frank Frisbie and
Harold Croft ordered the first .38 Special mould of Lyman's
with a hollow point, working out the plug size with Mr.
Pickering. This proved to be the most destructive .38
caliber bullet I have ever used on game. It expanded
readily with heavy loads of powder, and when cast as soft
as one to twenty, expanded perfectly if given a velocity of
1000 feet. This bullet is catalogued as Ideal #358429,
and as #358431 in the hollow-base version.

After considerable experimenting with these bullets in
several different guns, I have come to the conclusion that
the 160 grain weight is the best in this caliber, and that

one's choice lies between the hollow-base and the hollow-point, depending upon just how much destruction you wish. Both are extremely accurate at any range. The 160 grain weight can be given higher velocity than the 173 grain solid bullet. This added velocity more than makes up in actual killing power for the increased weight of the heavier bullet. The hollow-point seems to be the more popular of the two. With heavy loads of powder, it is altogether too destructive for grouse and similar table game as it blows them to pieces, but it is very suitable for pests, for lung shots on heavier game or where not too much penetration is required, I believe it would kill more quickly than the hollow-base 160 grain bullet. This 160 grain, Keith hollow-point, ahead of a heavy charge of powder, is the only .38 caliber bullet I have used that would kill a porcupine "dead" with one shot when hit through the paunch. I shot several of them out of big pine trees with such placing of shots and it seemed to kill instantly in all cases. Of course, the powder charge was heavy and was used in heavy, .45 frame Colt and Smith & Wesson guns. These bullets expanded to such an extent that they tore two inch holes at exit.

The uniformly excellent killing performed by these hollow-point bullets in .38 caliber, determined us to try them in the larger calibers as well, so we had Lyman hollow-point some moulds in both .44 Special and in .45 Colt. In the former, the regular Lyman hollow-point plug gave the bullet a weight of 235 grains, and by using this same size plug in the 250 grain .45 Colt mould, its weight was also cut to 235 grains. These weights are both better suited to high velocity loadings than were the 250 grain solid bullets. The solid bullets in all four calibers will penetrate more deeply but will not tear such unbelievably large holes in game as do the hollow-points. Since the .45 Colt bullet is the longest of the two in this caliber, I decided it would work out the best in hollow-point shape for both .45 Auto Rim and .45 Colt. The shooting by both Dickey

and myself, as well as many others we have handloaded it
for, proved it to be the most destructive of all .45 bullets.
A good many years ago a doctor from Michigan, I believe,
whose address I cannot remember, sent me samples of a
.45 Colt hollow-point bullet he had used for years with
black powder loads and with which he had obtained very
fine results. The cavity was very large, and, although he
used 40 grains of black powder, it expanded perfectly, even
on snowshoe rabbits. His bullet was of a round point style.
I cannot remember its weight. His experiments proved that
any sixgun bullet can be made to expand very reliably at
over 900 feet velocity with the proper size hollow-point
and correct temper to the alloy.

My designs of sixgun bullets have been so widely used
all over this country and Canada, and have proved so uniformly popular, that I honestly believe they will give as
good or better results than any design obtainable today.
They were designed for normal and heavy loads and not
for light, practice loads, still they have been used very
successfully by several fine target shots for gallery use with
light powder charges. Dr. Murphy of the Winnipeg Revolver Club made the possible score with my flat-base, 250
grain .44 Special bullet. They cut just as clean and full
holes in target paper as the commercial wad cutters do, and
at the same time have long, well-balanced points which will
shoot accurately to 500 yards, whereas most true, square-
fronted wad cutters begin to fall off in accuracy at any
range over 50 yards and often will show tipping on the
target at not much more than this. Other mould makers
have copied the design, and some individuals have tried
to revamp and rename the bullet by shortening its point or
changing the size of the hollow-point cavity, but so far I
have not seen any improvement on the original. Winchester and Major Wesson used this design in working out
the .357 Magnum. Their design is simply another variation from this bullet, but as it finally came out is more
nearly a copy of Ness's .45 Colt Bond bullet. Ness designed

this Bond hollow-base .45 Colt bullet several years before I worked out my designs with Lyman. My bullet is not the first with a flat point and square shoulder. Harry Pope used the same type of flat-point and wad-cutting forward band many years ago, and still uses it for his rifle bullets. However, the Keith bullet was the first one to incorporate a flat point; a wide, groove diameter band extending in front of the cartridge case; an adequate crimping groove; a wide, deep lubrication groove; a good and sufficient width of base band, and a dirt scraper-wad cutter—all on the one bullet.

Anyone who will take the time to recover his fired revolver bullets from snow, oiled sawdust, cotton waste or similar mediums which do not mutilate them, will immediately see that the greatest strains on the bearing bands of a sixgun bullet come on the front band. Look at the illustrations of fired bullets in Colonel Hatcher's excellent book on firearms identification. The bullet, traveling at high speed as it leaves the cylinder, jumps straight ahead into the barrel throat proper, there it skids about until it is gripped by the lands and forced to spin and rotate through the bore by them. Most of this skidding and slippage is taken up by the front band. The grooves left on it by the lands are generally always about twice as wide as normal, showing clearly that the bullet does strip this front band a bit before enough of its bearing surface has entered the barrel to hold it securely to the lands. By having a wide, groove diameter front band located in front of the crimp groove, we can cut this stripping and skidding to a minimum. Owing to the sharp, square shoulders and bands of these Keith bullets, they do not always drop from the mould cavity as easily as may those bullets with rounded bands and grooves, but those sharp shoulders are well worth the slight added work in casting; for one thing they will better scrape out the fouling left in the bore at each shot, a point much appreciated by the man using black powder.

For the man wanting a deeply seated bullet for use with a dense, fast powder in the .45 Colt, where the cases will be full length resized before reloading, the Ness-Bond bullet is a good one. It has proved very accurate and is also a good killer, possessing the same general type of flat point and front square-shoulder band as my bullets. It can be loaded to very high velocity also, using #2400 Hercules powder and has a long bearing surface necessary for finest accuracy at long ranges. The short, very blunt bullets usually do not work so well at long ranges as the longer ones, but even length can be overdone, as weight must be kept down to around the standard for that caliber for suitable long range accuracy. Too heavy a bullet raises pressures to such an extent that velocity must be kept very low, this in turn limits one's ability to hit relatively small objects at the longer ranges, due to the high trajectory.

Many shooters want to load the lightest possible bullet for extremely short range shooting, and for such purpose select the "collar button" bullets or a round ball. The latter worked best in the old percussion guns, which were cut with a slow gain twist and where the ball could be flattened out with the rammer to fill the cylinder. They may also be loaded in modern revolvers with very light charges of some really quick powder, like Bullseye. They are not as accurate as the collar button type and neither one is as good as a longer and heavier bullet for any purpose whatsoever. Frank Waterman loads round balls a great deal for his .45 Colt. These loads shoot quite accurately and are very cheap, but I for one prefer the longer, heavier weight. These light bullets and round balls, when used with extremely low charges, have a bad habit of bouncing back from any hard surface—or even a green tree trunk, for that matter, a situation which is not so favourable with me. Whenever I get down to this extreme "light" load stage, I generally go back to the ranch and break out one of my .22 handguns, which are much less expensive to

shoot and far less trouble to fix up with the most satisfactory sort of a light load.

The catalogues of the different bullet mould manufacturers in this country offer about every conceivable size and
shape of revolver bullet, and even the crankiest shooter
should be able to find something which suits him. My own
design suits me better than anything I have ever seen or
used, but it may not suit another individual at all and as
the Irishman said, "I believe in letting every man scratch
his own fleas in his own way."

CHAPTER FOUR

Bullet Casting

After deciding upon the weight and design of the bullet you wish to reload, the next step is to cast up an ample supply of that particular bullet. To obtain anything like proper results, it is necessary to possess a good melting pot and a dipper having a nozzle shaped to fit the pouring hole in the gate of your mould. The metal is best melted over a gas range, although very good work can be done with the kitchen stove, and I must admit having cast a great many more bullets in this way than over any gas range. We now use a gasoline blast furnace for bullet casting. This is at best a hot, hard job and one that few reloaders really care to perform.

The larger the melting pot, up to say twenty pounds capacity, the better, as a large pot will hold more metal and maintain a more uniform heat than it will with a smaller quantity of metal. First, melt the lead and when that is all melted add your tin or antimony. For most revolver cartridges, including all light and normal pressure loads, there is no use in having the bullets harder than one part tin to twenty parts of lead, and for really heavy loads, a one to fifteen mixture is hard enough. A very soft alloy is dangerous at over-normal loads, as the bullets will sometimes upset or swage out in the cylinder throat or barrel cone. This squashed-out, over-size slug can cause dangerous pressures and may split the rear end of the barrel. For automatic pistols, the bullets should be very hard, consisting of about one part tin to ten parts lead, in order for them to slide up easily out of the magazine into the chamber. The harder they are, the less they are apt to batter or catch on the corner or edge of the chamber. But such very hard, brittle bullets are not needed in any revolver load, except in the case of extreme penetration, where no upsettage or expansion is wanted.

Tin has a much lower melting point than lead but will not stand as much heat as antimony. For this reason antimony is often a better alloy than pure tin for use with very high velocity loads. A mixture of part tin and part antimony works very well indeed for some heavy loads. Hollow point bullets with velocities up to 1000 feet for proper expansion need not be over one part tin to twenty parts lead, and over that velocity it is best to use about a one-to-sixteen mixture.

After the lead is thoroughly melted, add the tin or tin and antimony mixture and let it melt and mix thoroughly. After the mixture has melted thoroughly, add a lump of tallow about half the size of a walnut and stir well in order to properly flux the metals. Then skim off all dross and dirt. Next, put a layer of fine charcoal on top; this prevents unnecessary burning and waste of the metal. The Ideal dipper works very well, but a much larger dipper made on the same pattern is still better. I have one made by H. W. Bradley, which holds about three times the quantity of metal as the Ideal, and does the best work of any ladle I have ever used. The more weight of metal there is in the dipper, the better it will force that metal into the mould, and at the same time exclude all air bubbles. Much finer quality bullets are obtained as a result of the process. The ladle must be kept very hot. I have found it advantageous to have a small stool or box set between myself and the gas furnace, and on a level with the top of the melting pot. After casting a bullet, the ladle handle can be laid down upon the box, with the hot bowl projecting over the pot of the metal. In this way the handle of the dipper stays comparatively cool.

It is best to warm up the moulds a bit at the side of the furnace or stove until they are comparatively hot, but still not hot enough for good work. Then add the final heating only by casting bullets. When the mould becomes hot enough to do really good work, it will usually require a few seconds for the metal to solidify in the sprue cutter. With hollow base or hollow point moulds, care will have to be exercised to allow them to cool longer than the solid bullets, or else the plug may tear out one side of the bullet if the moulds are jerked open too soon after pouring the metal. Use a wooden stick or light mallet to strike the gate with, and never allow any hard object to come in contact with the face of the mould. Special care must be taken not to use anything harder than the mould itself to cut off the sprue. Never allow anyone to dig a bullet out of the mould when it sticks in one of the halves. Tap the blocks gently with a soft stick until that bullet drops out. When a mould gets hot enough to do proper work, the bullets will generally drop out when it is opened suddenly. I have found that bronze moulds usually cast easier than iron moulds, why, I do not know. Bronze molds also are simpler to care for, and do not require greasing after using to protect from rusting.

In casting the bullet, hold the mould in the left hand, rotate it a quarter turn to the right so that the bullet cavity lays horizontal, then raise the dipper from the melting pot as nearly full of metal as practical, fit the nozzle to the cavity in the gate of the mould and slowly rotate both mould and ladle back to the left to a vertical plane. Now hold the mould and dipper in this position for a few seconds to allow plenty of time for the cavity in the mould to be completely filled before placing the dipper back over the pot. The main cause of uneven, partly filled bullets is the result of removing the dipper from the mould too soon and thus not allowing sufficient time for the cavity to fill. Remember, that after the cavity of the mould is filled, the metal shrinks as it hardens; therefore, the dipper should still be in place to allow the shrinking and cooling bullet to draw enough metal from the dipper for a few seconds to insure even, full weight bullets. Removing the dipper too soon will often cause the base band of the bullet to have uneven, partly filled, or rounded edges. To obtain accuracy, it is absolutely essential that all bands on the bullet be perfectly filled and sharp. In casting some 566 grain bullets for my old Buffalo Sharps, I must of necessity hold the ladle over the mould for a long time before removing it, or else the big slugs will have a rounded edge and quite often an air hole in the base.

With large caliber, heavy, sixgun bullets, if the moulds are hot (as they should be) and the sprue is still in a molten condition when the dipper is removed, it is well to add a little more metal to the "puddle" in the cavity of the gate, thus insuring perfect, evenly filled and full weight bullets. Many people think all that is necessary to cast bullets is to melt the lead in any kind of a ladle, then take an iron spoon and pour some metal in the mould until it is full. Although our ancestors did just this in running round balls for old percussion and flint lock rifles, it is next to, if not quite, impossible to secure perfect, modern revolver bullets from such methods.

Mould handles should always be long and cool. The most disagreeable bullet moulds of all to cast with are the short Colt, double ball, iron moulds furnished for the old percussion or cap and ball guns. The early, round ball, rifle moulds also usually had very short metal handles, and as soon as the moulds were hot enough to cast perfectly, they were too hot to hold in the bare hands. The old Ideal No. 4 with its bullet mould in the end of the loading tool and handles of metal is another type that soon gets too hot to hold while casting. The reason for

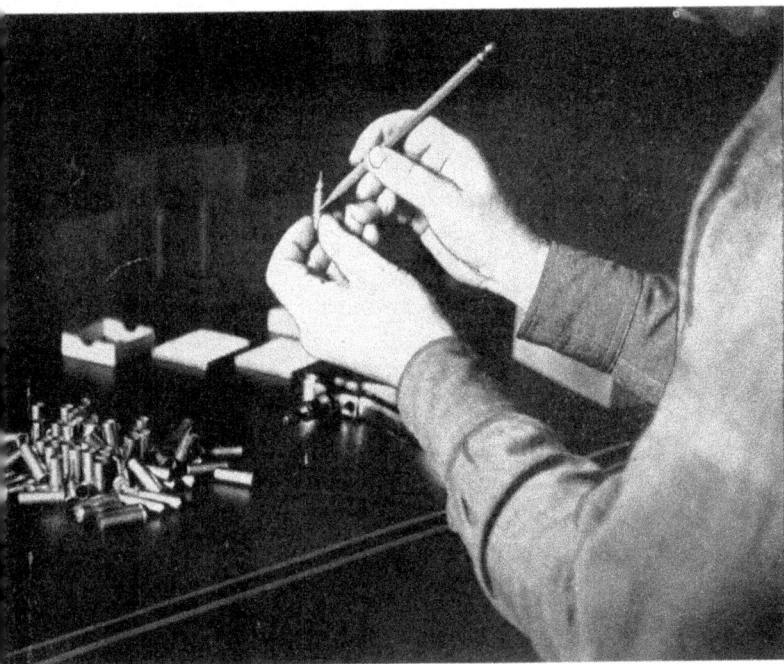

OPENING THE OLD CRIMP

All reloading tools provide one means or another for removing the old crimp and flaring or slightly belling the mouth of the fired case. The old Ideal tong type of tool employs its Cap Extractor for this purpose—and when properly adjusted, it turns out as neat a job as any of them.

In operating this tool, always use the proper size of decapping plug for the cartridge being decapped, do not try to "make out" with some Extractor made for a longer cartridge of the same caliber, as correct length is an important factor in this small but important appliance. Only the proper size Extractor can perform the two jobs of expelling the fired primer and flaring the case mouth at the one operation. Take time to properly adjust the Extractor in the loading chamber and this Ideal tool will do a splendid and speedy job of these two operations.

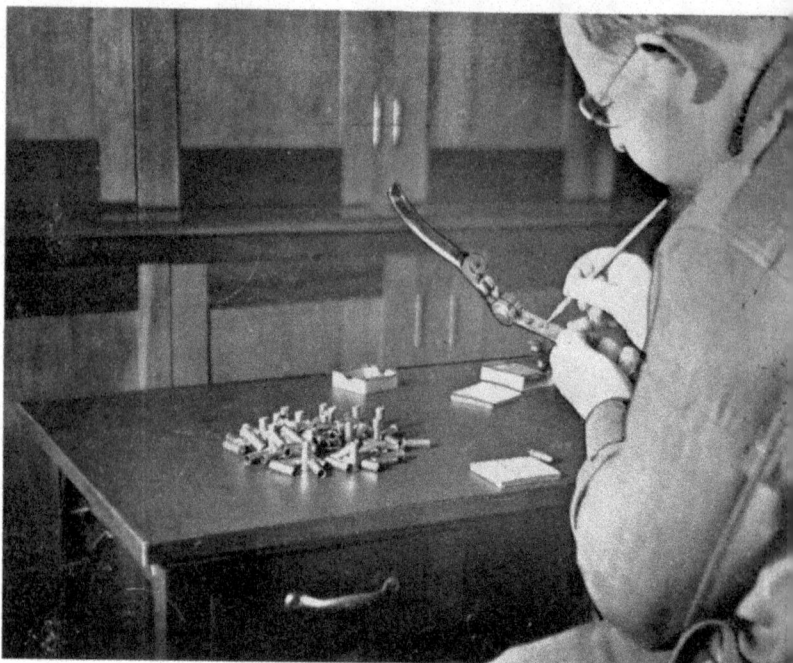

REPRIMING THE CASE

The lower priced hand tools cannot compare with the larger and more substantially built bench tools in many respects—but they have some features not possessed by these latter larger and more expensive apparatus. One of the great advantages of the tong tools is that they permit an easy and rapid inspection of the primer pockets while the new primer is being seated.

This is very important. The flash hole may have become clogged from corrosion; or what is more likely, with residue from the old primer as some of these non-corrosive primers leave considerable of an ash. Or else the front of the primer pocket may be cracked open or entirely blown out from repeated loading and firing. Close inspection of this primer pocket is essential and not many tools permit it being done as conveniently as the one shown above.

the Ideal No. 4, and all these very early light moulds, was to cut down weight as much as possible. In that day transportation was a serious problem and the less weight it would take to do the job the better, as those men were often gone for months with all their possessions on their back. If any additional weight was tolerated, it was wanted in more powder and lead, not in long, cool, but bulky and heavy bullet moulds. Many of these short, all metal moulds can be fitted with detachable handles that will afford adequate length and comfort in bullet casting. A pair of heavy cloth gloves is also a necessity at times, although I do most of this work bare-handed. Still and all, I acquire fewer burns when I wear cotton gloves all the time while casting bullets.

When casting over a kitchen range, the heat from the stove necessary to maintain an even temperature of the bullet metal, usually makes for very hot work. Generally, the women have asbestos mats of various sizes lying around to set hot pans on. (These can usually be obtained at any hardware store). I have found it advantageous to procure a number of these and stack them up all around the melting pot, in order to keep as much surplus heat as possible from rising up in one's face; this also helps maintain a more even temperature in the melting pot by sort of reflecting the heat or holding it where it is most wanted. When casting over a kitchen range, the work should be done in the cool of early morning or evening, or better still, on cold winter days. The firewood should be perfectly dry and split sufficiently fine to keep up a steady blaze. With coal to burn, the problem is easier once a good fire is going, but with some coal, such as that we get in the West, it is very hard to get a fire at all, let alone one sufficiently hot enough for bullet casting. The metal should never be too hot, as it then burns away and forms too much dross. It should, however, be hot enough —metal, dipper and mould, so that when a bullet is run it will require a few seconds for the sprue to solidify. Too hot a metal takes too long to solidify, often imparting a sort of galvanized or frosted finish to the bullet, and is also more apt to oxidize the mould inside until it will no longer cast good, smooth bullets.

The metal should be stirred from time to time, dipping deep in the pot and a little tallow added occasionally to flux, this of course, not always producing family harmony, as the good wife is very apt to wish that both yourself and that accursed smoking pot of metal were elsewhere. However, this is necessary for best results in bullet casting. Always dip the ladle or dipper down deep in the pot, as this helps to keep the metal evenly mixed. All bullet mixtures tend to change in temper as the metal is used up, so it is very hard to maintain the same proportion throughout an evening's bullet casting. The tin, antimony and lead should be carefully weighed for best results and not merely guessed at.

The charcoal over the top helps to keep the metal clean and free from dross. Any dross in the dipper will often be deposited on the sides or base of the bullet causing it to be unevenly balanced. This kind of bullet should be discarded. When the melting pot gets too hot, the metal usually turns a blue color. Fire should then be cut down somewhat, as it will only oxidize and burn up the metal fast. Extreme heat also tends to change the temper of the alloy to some extent.

A new mould is often quite a task to break in, but the one best way to do it is to keep on casting bullets. At times, it is well to grease the mould inside with a little tallow when hot and then continue casting until the bullets begin to drop out on opening the mould. Of course, after greasing the mould will cast only wrinkled bullets until all traces of the grease are burned out of the blocks, but when this is accomplished, it will often cast much better. Occasionally the addition of a little lump of grease to the mixture and a thorough stirring of the metal, also helps make the casting of perfect bullets an easier task, as well as keeping the metals better mixed.

Great care must be exercised in not allowing water or moisture to collect about a bullet mould or melting pot while casting, as water in a pot of molten metal acts like fire to a Giant Powder cap, and will precipitate hot lead all over the surrounding scenery. Caution must be used in adding odd bits of metal to the pot, especially old lead pipe in the winter time, as it may contain some ice inside. All such old metal should first be heated up or preferably put in the pot while the latter is cold so that both pot and metal will be brought to the right temperature together. Another sure-fire way of producing excitement, to say nothing of bad burns, is to drop a loaded cartridge in the melting pot along with a quantity of recovered bullets that you wish to melt up, as Lemuel Smelzer once did while working with me at Durkee, Oregon. My face, hands, arms and shirt front were completely covered with melted metal, as well as Mrs. Keith's cookstove and the walls of the kitchen. Both of my eyes burned, and it was some time before I could see at all. Needless to say, I got hot under the collar in more ways than one.

Some moulds are very cranky and it may take considerable steady casting before they will throw good bullets, then again they may suddenly begin to throw bum and imperfect bullets after having cast perfect ones for hours. Sometimes the trouble will result from the metal being too hot or too cool. Other times, it seems to be nothing but pure unadulterated cussedness on the part of the mould, and one will simply have to keep working along until the mould again casts properly. At such times, I often grease the mould inside, and then cast until the grease burns out completely, a process which often starts the mould casting good again.

There may be times, after a mould has been used a great

deal or has been heated too greatly from continuous casting when the metal was entirely too hot, that the cavity will become oxidized and will cast rough looking bullets, the points or an edge of the bands of which will not fill out at all. In mild cases, this is usually cured by dropping a small bit of tallow in the mould, then continue casting until the mould has burned out all of the grease. This procedure is usually successful. In aggravated cases this will sometimes fail to do the trick, as such was the case with Dickey and me last evening. The mould will then have to be repolished inside to remove the oxidization. Most printers use Putch's Pomade for mould polishing, but this is often very difficult, if not quite impossible to obtain, particularly by those individuals living back on the ragged edges of civilization. We have found that powdered pumice stone works about as well, cutting out the oxidization quickly and repolishing the mould cavity.

The safest way to do this is to take a full and sharp bullet—one which perfectly fits the mould—place it in the cavity and grip the handles until it is held firmly. After doing this, take a small punch and mark it in the exact center. Now take a small breast drill and drill down in the center about half the length of the bullet, being very careful to hold the drill vertically. While a friend checks one side, you check from the other angle. Next take a small machine screw, turn it down into the cavity in the bullet thus formed and you have a real "polishing head." This can be rotated or turned by a screw driver twirled between the palms of the hands, but it is best to cut off the head of the screw and chuck it in the breast drill. Then coat the bullet with light oil and some powdered pumice stone, and while a friend or helper holds the mould halves together with a steady, even tension, but not tight enough to bind the bullet and prevent its rotating, spin the bullet around and around until the mould is thoroughly polished. This will usually require but a few minutes, and after the mould has been used enough to burn out the oil, it will again cast perfectly. Of course, the mould should be thoroughly cleaned after the polishing, before again casting. This can be best done with gasoline.

Sometimes a mould may refuse to do good work, because of trapped air imprisoned in the cavity when the metal is poured into it. In this case, the mould will have to be vented. Very few workmen can properly vent a mould as could Harry Pope and other of the fine old Scheutzen rifle makers, most of whom, with the exception of Pope and Peterson, are now dead. However, there are ways of accomplishing this yourself, always two ways to skin a cat remember. The mould, if for a solid bullet, can be vented by merely making a very slight scratch on the face of one block back about one-eighth to one-fourth inch from the cavity, and as near as possible to that portion of the cavity that refused to fill out properly. The slight burr thrown up by a tiny knife cut or scratch will usually allow the imprisoned air to escape and the mould to still cast perfectly. With hollow point moulds, the best system I have found is to take a pair of small ordinary pliers, and with the rear portion of the jaws, (used for small wire cutting) grip the plug down next to its handle so that the point to be cut or marred will be about half way between the mould cavity and the outside of the mould. Holding the pliers fairly tight on this hollow point plug stem, rotate it with the fingers and thus make a small cut around it. This will throw up a slight burr, which spreads the mould just enough to allow the air to escape, but not enough, however, to allow the molten metal to flow out between the mould faces and make an angel out of your bullet. The above stunts will usually cure any balky mould, but they must be done carefully or the mould can be ruined very easily.

Some folks think that a mould is useful as a pair of pliers. I have had some thoughtless individuals to use my moulds to pull nails, etc. when I was not at home. Such practices come under the same classification as the cow puncher who uses the front sight of his sixgun to pull staples and then, after leading his nag over the wire while he stands on it, drives them in again with the butt of the gun. Such people use the top of their heads merely as a hat rack, possessing nothing but solid ivory above the ears.

Use as light a pine stick as possible to strike the gate and cut the sprue off the bullet, as many moulds have too light and too thin a swinging gate (including the Lyman) which sooner or later will not be struck perfectly square and will bend, with the result that your bullet will turn into an angel and have wings on the base. Sometimes the gate or sprue cutting plate will warp from the heat. When this happens, they must then be placed on a perfectly flat surface plate and trued up again, a job which is at best difficult unless one is properly equipped to do it.

Where possible to do so, bullet casting should be done during the cold of winter, as it is then a much more pleasant job than on a hot summer day. The work table or bench should be handy to the worker, so that he can drop the bullets out without having to move about too much. The top of the table or bench should be covered with several thicknesses of cloth, burlap or old blankets to cushion the bullets when they fall, as they are very easily upset or battered when they come hot from the mould, being very soft and not thoroughly hardened.

When through casting with any iron mould, it should always be greased while still hot, and the best way to do this is to leave the last bullet in the cavity and drop some grease on the base of the said bullet, or point, if it is a point cut-off mould. Belding & Mull make moulds of solid nickel, while the Yankee Specialty Co. make theirs of bronze. These latter bronze moulds are very good and cast fine bullets with the least effort of any I have used. They also make a 255 grain bullet for the .44 Special that gives wonderful accuracy for me at extreme ranges, although being a round nose bullet it has little stopping power. The Lyman system affords the reloader a great many different moulds with one set of handles. It takes but a few minutes time to change blocks, so that the handloader can purchase several sets of mould blocks for different bullets, yet with their new type moulds needs but the one set of handles.

After the cast bullets are thoroughly cool, go over them and select the perfect ones for use and throw the imperfect bullets back in the pot for remelting. All told, this bullet casting is by far the hardest job of hand reloading.

CHAPTER FIVE

Bullet Sizing and Lubricating

Now that we have a plentiful supply of bullets cast up for use during the next few months' shooting, we can proceed with the operations of sizing and lubricating. First of all though, it may be wise to examine into the bore of the sixgun these bullets will be fired through and ascertain beyond the shadow of a doubt just what its cylinder and groove dimensions happen to be. I know of many shooters who have been using all sorts of revolvers for years, yet who have never yet taken the trouble to determine this most vital point.

Clamp your sixgun into a vise which has its jaws suitably padded to prevent marring, gun with muzzle vertical. Now take a soft lead bullet, start it point first down the muzzle of the gun and tap it on into the bore, using a small stick of hardwood as a drift and tapping that with a mallet or hammer. Be careful to drive it in as straight with the axis of the bore as possible. After it goes down flush with the muzzle of the gun it may upset or flare out at the base. Pay no attention to this but take a hardwood cleaning rod and drive that bullet on through the barrel, having first opened the cylinder or removed it from the gun. If you do not happen to have a suitable vise around, you can hold the gun in your hand or between your knees while the bullet is being forced through. As the bullet emerges, catch it with the fingers or on some folds of cloth laid in the cylinder recess of the frame.

Now we have a bullet which, if it has been properly driven through the bore, will give us the exact groove diameter of that particular barrel, which is what we are interested in. Hold the bullet in your left hand by its point and turn your micrometer up on its base and middle bands, using only the rachet to turn with. Any Colt gun will be easy to mike, as they have six grooves and lands. Remember that the "lands" on that bullet are the groove diameter of your barrel. Mike both base and front or middle bands, being sure to take the readings from the widest part of the bullet. In other words, make certain your micrometer is bearing on the center of the band on each side. With Smith & Wesson guns and their five groove barrels, this is a harder job, as one must mike from the edge or corner of one land across to the edge of the corner opposite. If done carefully, they can be miked all right, but they are harder to do than the Colt barrels.

It might be advisable to repeat the slugging operation and shove another soft bullet through the gun a second time—then check against the first readings. After having ascertained this groove dimension beyond any doubt, it might also be well to repeat the process and determine the diameter of the cylinder throats. This is not so important as the groove diameters, but it is well to know for certain that these throats are not smaller than the barrel grooves, a situation which I have often known to be the case with the older .45 Colt Single Actions. Take a full-sized bullet, as it comes from the mould, and make certain it can be pushed through the cylinder throats without any difficulty; or, if you want to "slug" them properly, upset a soft bullet in each throat and then mike these accurately.

Now we are ready to proceed with the sizing of the bullet, and possibly its lubricating at the same time. With light loads and comparatively light, short bullets, the diameter of the sized bullet can be as much as .003″ over groove diameter of your barrel, but with normal and heavy loads I much prefer that those bullets be sized to not more than .002″ over our groove diameter. This .002″ is the diameter over groove measurements which I prefer for most sixgun loads, although as elsewhere stated, for large caliber guns of .44 and .45 caliber a difference of .001″ is not so important as in the smaller .38 caliber guns. Thus, in the .44 Special and .45 Colt you can get by with a diameter of .003″ over groove diameter easier than you can in a .38 Special or smaller caliber. Even a diameter of but .001″ over groove diameter seems to shoot with extreme accuracy and I prefer such a sizing of bullets for maximum or magnum loads, especially in the heavy frame .38 caliber guns. My S. & W. Magnum measures .357″ groove diameter and I size my bullets for it to .358″.

Most of the Smith & Wesson .44 Special guns I have slugged and miked, ran .430″ groove diameter and I size all bullets for these guns to .431″. Most of the Colt guns I have tried, and there have been a great many, have shown groove diameters of .4265″ to .4285″ and for these guns I generally size the bullets to .429″. With some early .44/40 Colts which have since been fitted with .44 Special cylinders, I have found the groove diameters to run as small as .423″ to .424″, and for such the bullets should be sized down to .425″ or .426″ and any larger diameter should never be tolerated. There is no "hoss-sense" whatever in trying to resize your lead bullets ahead of some 15,000 to 25,000 pounds pressure in the thin walled cylinders of your revolver. Furthermore, I have seldom seen any accuracy obtained from the use of bullets greatly in excess of the groove diameter of the gun.

As I said before, care should be taken to see that your sized bullet will always shove through the throat of the cylinder chambers of the gun, by hand and using but little effort. Many .45 guns, especially the older, very early production, will be found with barrels having groove diameters of only .450″ to .452″ and the chambers will be found correspondingly small, while with other guns, especially those assembled from old parts (and there are thousands of these assembled guns floating around), the cylinder throats may mike only .450″ while the bore may be as much as .454″ or even .455″. Such a combination is hopeless for accuracy until you have had those chamber throats reamed out to .001″ over groove diameter. I have had some Colt guns which had a cylinder throat measurement of .457″ and a groove diameter of .452″. Such a combination cannot give proper results, and the best cure for such cases is a new cylinder. Any cylinder having extremely large chamber-mouth measurements is also mighty apt to be chambered oversize. This extreme variation amongst the .45 Colt clan, as well as the fact that similar variations seemed to exist in most loading tools made for it, was one of the reasons why I quit the .45 caliber in favor of the .44 Special as my heavy caliber cartridge.

The late J. D. O'Meara was an exceptionally skillful workman on .45 Colt guns, as he thoroughly understood all of these facts. He reamed out several .45 Colt cylinders for me and also fitted new barrels to some of the guns. Some of the finest shooting .45 Colts in existence in the West today are those which that fine old scout worked over and fitted up. The men now owning those guns should be proud of them. He had but one hand to work with and how he ever turned out such good work with only that one "mitt" has always been a mystery to me.

Now that we have figured out the exact diameter to which our bullet must be sized, we can get along to the actual performance of the job itself. By far the best method, and the cheapest in the long run, is to obtain one of the Lyman Ideal or the Modern Bond bullet sizers and lubricators. These machines are splendid and there is nothing that can quite take their place for doing the combined job of sizing and lubricating—which they do at the one operation. Either firm can furnish you with extra dies for any caliber, or to any measurement you may desire, as well as supply you with an exceptionally good grade of stick lubricant in proper size to fit their machines. I cannot recommend too strongly that the handloader obtain one of these sizing and lubricating machines. There is nothing to equal them as a time and labor saver, or to do as perfect a job, provided the proper dies and punches are arranged and properly regulated in the machine. Get one of these machines by all means so that you may avoid a lot of trouble.

If the beginner cannot afford one of these machines, then fairly good results can be obtained with the Ideal or Belding & Mull small, hand bullet sizers. The Ideal should be obtained in the *base-first* type which screws into their #3 or similar loading tool in place of the loading chamber. These dies may be had in any diameter, they being very accurate, but the bullet must first be lubricated by hand before it can be sized. For this lubricating, about the best method I have found is to take a very shallow pan or pot and in it melt up enough lubricant for the job. Use either a prepared lubricant like the Ideal Banana, or a home-brew article of beeswax and tallow, or even pure beef tallow can be made to do.

Take a pair of fairly long tweezers or pliers and gently grasp the point of the bullet, then immerse its base into the melted lubricant as deeply as necessary, at least deep enough to cover all its lubrication grooves. Lift it out and stand it on its base on a clean, planed board. A still better method, is to stand all your bullets on their bases in the shallow pan and then pour melted lubricant around them until it is above the level of the top groove, or as deep as you want it. After the lubricant has hardened, take an Ideal Kake Kutter, or similar gadget made at home by cutting the head off a suitable rifle cartridge and expanding its neck until it will just slip over the base of the bullet, and thrust it down over the point of each bullet, one after another, until the "slicked off" bullets work out the top of the tool.

They are now ready to be put through the *base-first* hand-sizing die. After this is done, all surplus grease should be carefully wiped off the points of the bullets, as well as from their bases—take the time to do this last, because it may affect the powder charge or cause a squib. Any grease left on the point of the bullet will only gum up the loading chamber of the tool or cause trouble from seating it and the following bullets at too great a depth in the case. After cleaning, pack your finished bullets away neatly, using some small covered box or similar container and standing them all base down and against each other so that their lubricant will not spread all over adjoining bullets, and so they will be protected from dirt and grit, elements which promptly adhere to the greased bullet *and stay there*.

While on this subject of bullet sizing, I want to say a word or two regarding those old Ideal tools which had a hole drilled through their lower handle with a swinging punch in the upper handle, for the alleged purpose of sizing bullets. I have never yet found one of these tools with a sizing hole which was ROUND; also that punch invariably strikes the bullet base off-center, badly upsetting, and in many cases, bending the bullet while forcing it through that hole. Such tools are a joke and will only ruin already excellent bullets, which almost always shoot more accurately just as they come from the mould than they do after being shoved through any such excuse for a bullet sizer. If you have such a tool, get a separate bullet sizer of the *base-first* type, or if your tool has the double-adjustable, removable chamber, order the base-first sizing die and chamber to fit it and good results will be obtained. Never attempt to correctly size bullets through one of those makeshift sizing holes in an old combination tool. During the last War, every Ideal tool I was able to procure had an oval shaped bullet sizing hole. For serious revolver shooting, all bullets must be accurately and perfectly sized to fit the individual gun.

The price of the Ideal or Bond machine will soon be justified by the saving in time, as well as by the added convenience and accuracy of its use and the elimination of all surplus grease from the bullet and hands. When lubricating bullets by hand, I always get some of that grease on my clothes as well, and my nose never fails to itch just about the time my hands get greased well and good—everything manages to get well lubricated by the time the job is finished. Then in using gas-check bullets, which are sometimes used with the .32/20 or .44/40 calibers to advantage with stiff loads, these machines work beautifully. Start that gas-check on the bullet base and seat it into the die. The top lever sends it down the required depth and when the bullet is pressed against the bottom punch the gas-check is permanently and *squarely* affixed. This is a hard trick to do without the machine, for they have to be started on the bullet base with the fingers and then tapped with a mallet or piece of wood while the bullet is held in the fingers. It is hard to force them on squarely and yet great care must be exercised to do this or else you will have a bullet with a slanting base, a situation which is never conducive to accuracy. The powder gases cannot be depended upon to force them on evenly as the bullet base or copper cup may be upset from the tapping, or shock of discharge, or the friction as it enters the barrel. In the .32/20 cartridge, these gas-checks are a great help with some powders for heavy loads, as they greatly cut down the chances for fusion of the bullet base, also the edge of those hard metal cups seem to scrape the bore clean with each shot, eliminating leading to a great extent, even with the very high velocity loads. I have always had very satisfactory results when loading gas-check bullets in my .32/20 S. A. Colt.

Leading of sixgun barrels is usually caused by too hot a powder, by an oversized or an undersized bullet, or by too heavy a charge of powder. With the heavy loads of #2400 Hercules powder that I have mentioned, some leading will occur at times in perfect and well polished barrels. Such charges are bound to be fairly hot, as the bullet is driven up the bore at such high speed that the friction alone may cause some leading. Plenty of good, graphite impregnated lubricant is usually sufficient to stop this. But I remember one time, when using very heavy charges of Bullseye in an old S. A. Colt .32/20, that the gun leaded badly with either hard or soft bullets, due to the extremely hot powder fusing their bases. I tried everything to stop this and finally with gas-check bullets I had no more trouble. With plain base bullets, however, the leading continued every time I exceeded the normal load of Bullseye. Finally, I obtained a box of dental wax from a dentist and tried cutting wads out of this by pressing a sheet of it over the case after loading the powder and before seating the bullet. This was fifteen years ago.

By so loading the dental wax, it seemed to eliminate the leading. No doubt it prevented the hot flame from reaching the base of the bullet. I tried to use thin card wads on the base of those bullets, but these would not stay in place in the slightly bottle-necked .32/20 cases, so I used the dental wax most of the time. I also tried using the dental wax next to the powder and the thin card wad next to the bullet base. This stunt worked the best of anything except the copper gas-check bullets.

No doubt the present graphite or impregnated grease wads sold for use in the .22/4000 rifles would help reduce leading in sixguns, but I have not tried them. I discovered that even #5 is too hot for heavy doses. I sent Major Wesson a 230 grain Keith hollow base bullet fired from my S & W, triple lock, .44 Special that went lengthwise through a coyote at 50 yards with 7.5 grains #5. The yellow dog turned around with a yelp when that bullet struck him in the chest and then piled up. I recovered the bullet from a snow bank in back of the coyote. That bullet still showed the base band badly fused on the outside, and this in spite of its hollow base which, some would have us believe, always spreads or swages out to completely fill up the bore.

Most bullet moulds are cut large enough to throw an oversized bullet and thus insure its working properly through the sizing die; hence almost any bullet as cast will be oversized for the average sixgun barrel; therefore there is a necessity for sizing tools or machines to swage or size down bullets to the proper diameter. Some bullets might come from the mould in proper size to lubricate and use. Many of the Schuetzen rifle bullets are made this way and need only to be lubricated. However, it is much the best to resize all revolver bullets. Any mould which casts an undersized bullet should be promptly returned to the factory or thrown away, for it cannot be properly re-sized or lubricated, as the grease will squeeze out along the sides and make a very messy job of things. Further-more, undersized bullets are apt to gas cut and lead badly. This condition prohibits them from developing satisfactory accuracy.

With all the bullet sizing dies, whether the base-first accessory of the tong tools or the much better sizing and lubricating machines, it is essential to use a top punch which *exactly* fits the point or nose of the bullet being worked. Do not try to extemporize or make some other top punch do, because these top punches hold the bullet in a true line while it is being forced into the die and help turn out a perfectly centered bullet. With improperly fitting top punches, the bullet will be shoved to one side or the other and its axis forced out of line with the base. Also see to it that the base of the bullet seats squarely in the die, so that it will not be upset and the bullet ruined. Keep both the inside of the top punch and the top of the base punch wiped clean of surplus grease, and be sure to adjust the seating depth of the machine so that the bullet will be shoved clear down into its sizing die and will have all of its bands properly sized, particularly the front band. Do not have any lubricant ahead of the front band.

Too much care cannot be exercised in the preparation of your bullets. Regardless of how much care and skill you employ in loading the cartridge, you will not get

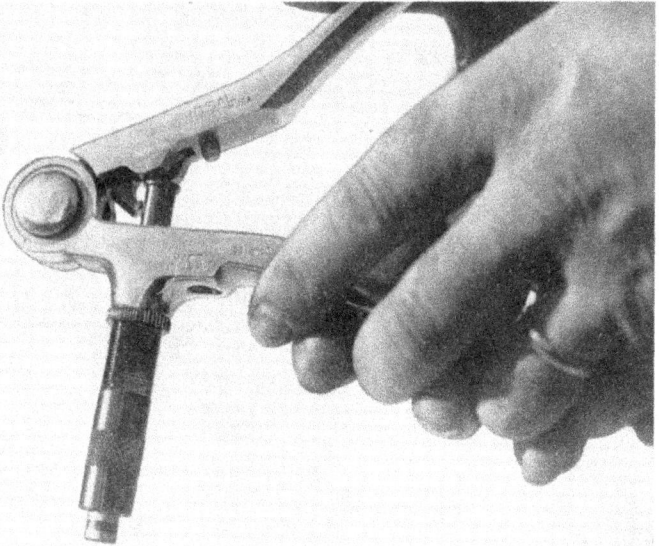

SIZING THE BULLET

Accurate sizing of the lubricated bullet is important and only precision dies should be employed. The bullet should always be forced base first into or through the die. The above illustration shows latest model Ideal Sizing Chamber being employed—this type should be used in preference to the older tool where only a sizing hole was furnished and the bullet shoved through point first.

This Ideal Bullet Sizing Chamber can also be used independently of the tool. When used separately, it works on the same principle as the Belding & Mull bullet sizer.

CHARGING THE PRIMED CASES

Illustration shows a logically arranged set-up for accurately measuring out normal charges of a powder such as Hercules Bullseye. Workbench cleared of all unnecessary tools and the Ideal measure clamped on a convenient but solid foundation. The primed cases are taken, one at a time, from the loading block on the left, (where they have been placed base up and previously inspected for protruding or mashed primers) the charge thrown directly from the measure and the loaded case then slipped into the loading block on the right. After again being carefully inspected (for double charges) bullets are placed in position and crimped with the hand loading tool.

accuracy unless you have perfect bullets which are the correct diameter for your individual gun.

For practice shooting, one can shoot into large blocks of wood or better still into one of these patented bullet stops with target holder attached, and thus save all of your lead for remelting. Use of these will greatly cut down the cost of such shooting. For the last five years I have been using a Koehler Brothers bullet stop, both for target practice and for sighting in guns for folks who come here for a visit or to get their gun sighted up. This excellent back stop catches all the lead, and it is surprising the amount of bullet metal I take out of it during a year's time and save for future use. It is also much more handy to clip a target on the front of this Koehler backstop than to mess around hunting up tacks and using a block of wood, furthermore the back may be removed from this bullet stop in a very few minutes and the bullet metal easily taken out.

CHAPTER SIX

Revolver Powders

We have today, quite a variety of satisfactory revolver powders to select from and the handloader can obtain almost any velocity he desires by using the proper brand. For light to normal charges, Bullseye is a splendid powder. It is especially useful in very light, gallery or practice loads where only a pinch is required. Its charges run so light and the load bulks up so small in the case that it is one of the cheapest of all pistol powders to use. It is exceptionally accurate, even in very light charges, and best of all, it ignites easily. No matter how much air space remains in the case or how poor or irregular the crimp is, just as long as a good smokeless primer is used, Bullseye will do its stuff. It is a very fastburning, hot powder and will burn completely and cleanly in very short barrels. Pressures are highly uniform if care is used in loading. Bullseye is not a good powder for any but light to normal loads, as it is too hot and will fuse the base of the bullet if extreme charges are attempted. The base band will melt badly long before the maximum pressure is arrived at.

Undoubtedly the greatest handicap in using Bullseye is the ease with which two charges can be loaded into the same case. The powder is so condensed and so little is required for even normal loads that a double charge can readily be thrown and the bullet seated with no trouble, in fact, the trouble only comes when that double charge is fired. Bullseye has a balance point around 9000 pounds pressure, with a satisfactory working range extending some 4000-5000 pounds below and only some 3000 pounds above this point. It has what might be termed a medium working range and is so dense a powder that extreme care should always be used in its loading. It is a very accurate, reliable powder and is extremely stable.

The newer duPont Pistol Powder #5 is a bit better powder for average loads than Bullseye. It bulks up some-what better in the case and a double charge is more easily detected. In any case, however, extreme care must be exer-cised in loading any of the dense pistol powder in order to avoid this trouble. Being a nitrocellulose powder, #5 is not quite as hot burning as Bullseye, but it does not possess the ease of ignition of this latter brand. It has a wider working range and a balance point of about 10,000 pounds. #5 works well in light loads, probably in not quite as small charges as Bullseye, but it can be used in charges slightly over normal without running into too great trouble. Still, it is too hot and quick burning for heavy loads and will fuse bullet bases before the maximum safe pressure can be reached in the heavy frame guns.

The duPont Company recently put out a new pistol powder known as #6, it is a brand which I am as yet unfamiliar with but my friends report it to be a splendid and very accurate powder. F. C. Ness told me it gave better average accuracy than the older #5 and had a wider tolerance and working range.

The above three brands are the smokeless powders which the beginner should start off with—after he has had a bit of experience with black powder. Carelessness must not be tolerated when the charges are being thrown in the cases, and a close inspection should be made of each block full of charged cases before the bullets are seated. Use only the proper smokeless primers and don't attempt any "cocktail" loads or fancy black-powder-priming stunts until you have gotten the hang and swing of things. After which, say six months or a year of such loading and shooting, you will be qualified to take up the loading of the following powders:

Hercules Unique is a fine powder for loads slightly above normal on up to the full pressures the arm will safely stand. It is not nearly as good for magnum revolver loads as their #2400, but is a fine powder up to 15,000 or 16,000 pounds, giving very good velocities for the pressures developed. I consider it a much better powder than duPont #80 for heavy and medium heavy revolver loads but it has a narrow working range and is also a very hot, nitroglycerin powder like Bullseye; accordingly, one must load carefully with a close check on pressures. Unique is a fine powder for loads around 1000 feet velocity, getting close to 1100 feet in some cases with normal weight bullets. The magnum loads are not obtained with it as well as with #2400, as its heat fuses the bases when overloaded. I do not consider it a suitable powder for light loads.

Unique best takes the place of #80 powder, giving about the same velocities that may be obtained with the latter but with less pressure and with less variation in pressures. In some cases it will give results better than are obtainable with any other powder. I like it very well for loads in the .45 Auto Rim. Unique has a balance point around 13,000 pounds, with a working range of about 4000 pounds above this, but very little below. It is a very accurate and thoroughly stable powder and a reliable brand to use if the charge is properly fitted to the cartridge and due care exercised in its loading.

For a good many years duPont #80 powder was our best bet for heavy revolver loads, in spite of criticisms by many handloaders. Properly loaded, it will give very fine accuracy at comparatively high velocity. I do not like it as well as Unique for many loads, mainly on account of its being affected by moisture or extremes in temperature. It will dry out if stored in a hot place. Also, the permissible charge may vary as much as two grains in different lots of this powder, this being a big variation for some cartridges.

Cartridges loaded with #80 and stored in a hot and dry climate may in a short time so increase in pressure that they are decidedly unsafe, hence this powder should be loaded for immediate use and not stored away. This fact, that it will dry out and greatly increase in power and pressure under some storage conditions, makes it an unsafe powder for revolvers under all conditions of loading. At times, loads worked out and carefully checked at low temperatures become altogether too strong for use in hot weather.

DuPont #80 has a balance point around 16,000 pounds, which is above the safety line for many revolver cartridges, yet well within the limits of safety of our better made, heavy frame .44 Special revolvers or in .38 Special guns on .45 frames. It does not burn well unless loaded to near the maximum safe pressure and will squib badly at times in lighter charges. But properly loaded, for near or immediate use in heavy charges, with these charges properly worked up and the loading carefully controlled, it will give a good account of itself. Unless loaded in full charges, there will be considerable unburned powder left in the bore of the gun and even in maximum loads it does not burn any too completely. It will not give as good velocities as will Hercules #2400 in magnum and maximum charges in such cartridges as the .38 Special, .44 Special and .45 Colt, yet it works well in all these calibers and is very good in the .45 Auto Rim. The .32/20, .38/40 and .44/40 take well to it, but higher velocities, with the same or less pressure, can be obtained with #2400.

I know of several good Officer's Model Colts being blown up with a charge of 11 grains of #80 behind the standard 158 grain bullet. In order to find out the pressure this load developed, I loaded some and used them in my S & W Outdoorsman with fine accuracy and great killing power. Knowing them to be greatly in excess of maximum safe loads for the .41 frame guns, I sent some to Peters for test and my friend Col. Tewes reported an average pressure of 42,000 pounds. It was no wonder that those Officer's Models let go. I do not consider #80 a safe powder nor a good one for any light frame revolver. In the .45 Colt it will work well up to a charge of 15 grains with my 250 grain Lyman bullet, provided the bullet diameter is carefully checked and the bullet properly and well crimped in the crimp groove. Over this charge, I am off #80 in the .45 Colt and with good reason, because with 16.3 grains and my 260 grain Belding & Mull .45 Colt bullet, I cracked the rear end of the barrel in three places.

My friend Ashley Haines has obtained wonderful results with #80 in both the .45 Colt and the .44/40 Single Action. However, he is a very careful handloader who thoroughly knows what it is all about. I had good results with this powder in the .38/40. But recent shooting has shown me that with less velocity it will expand the cases more than does #2400. Since the advent of this latter Hercules powder, I am through with #80 in revolvers.

Hercules #2400 is the powder used by Winchester in working up the .357 Magnum cartridge, and to my notion it is the best of all powders for extreme or maximum loads in heavy frame, thick cylindered revolvers. This powder will not work well in anything but heavy loads and if these loads are crowded too much it will fuse the bullet somewhat, causing leading; still I believe most of the leading one obtains from this powder to be due to friction from the greatly increased velocity. Keep in mind that right after we took to using smokeless powder in rifles and obtained above 1500 feet velocity, we had to go to the metal cased bullet because of stripping and leading. #2400 does not develop as high pressures for the same velocity as does #80 and seems to be a much more suitable powder, certainly results may be obtained in the .38

Special, .44 Special and .45 Colt which cannot be equalled with any other powder I know of.

This #2400 is no powder for the novice to use in reloading pistol ammunition. Very fine high velocity loads, however, may be worked up by the experienced handloader and with it maximum killing and stopping power will be developed. For use in the .38 Special cartridge to be fired only in guns like the .45 frame Colt or heavy S & W, we load a charge of 13.5 grains of #2400 with the 160 grain Keith Lyman bullet and get killing results that are not to be obtained with any other combination in this cartridge. In the .44 Special we load 18.5 grains with my 235 grain hollow point bullet and with the .45 Colt we use the Keith 235 grain hollow point and 22 grains of #2400. Loads such as these should only be put up in new, heavy cases in perfect condition. They will at any rate give you the maximum power in these calibers. In the .357 Magnum S & W revolver we load 15 grains of #2400 and the 160 grain Keith Lyman bullet. With all the loads listed in this paragraph, the bullet diameter is fixed at .001″ to not more than .002″ over groove diameter and cast to a temper of one part tin to sixteen parts lead, or a mixture of half tin and half antimony in the same Bill Bryan formula.

I have tried to work out a good load in the .45 Auto Rim case with #2400, but have not been successful, the powder seemingly developing the maximum permissible pressure long before it reaches a clean burning stage. This #2400 powder seems to work best in the longer revolver cases and the .45 Colt charges I have mentioned throughout this book are intended for the standard, long Colt shell and not any of those short, Remington, squib cases.

With all revolver loads, it must be kept in mind that you are working with pressures which must be held under a certain definite point and when you go over such pressures the gun may go to pieces. You do not have the margin of safety such as exists in loading rifle cartridges, where a grain or so too much may mean only a pierced or blown out primer with possibly a spurt of gas in the face; in the sixgun such action would probably wreck the arm. The powder charges in a revolver cartridge are small in proportion to modern rifle charges, consequently an increase of a fraction of a grain in the handgun may raise pressures much more in proportion than would a two grain increase in the rifle. Therefore, act accordingly.

In preparing light or normal cartridges, the charges may be loaded very satisfactorily by using the Belding & Mull, Lyman or similar powder measures, first carefully checking the measure settings with an accurate scale. Don't put too much faith in the corner or village drug store scales for this or any other powder weighing. I have seen several druggist's balances which were far better adapted to weighing brickbats than small powder charges. A Fairbanks assay scale, the Troemner or other standard balances, or the Pacific powder scales are to be relied on.

When you come to loading any of my recommended charges of either #80 or #2400 powders, each and every one of these loads should be weighed by hand to one-tenth of a grain—at least try to get them that close—and then use these cartridges ONLY in the heavy framed revolvers of Smith & Wesson and Colt make.

For the average beginner in handloading there is nothing quite so safe as black powder. True, it is dirty, and smoky, and fouls bore and cases badly until both have to be cleaned with hot water or solvent, but a lot of fun, satisfaction and *experience* can *safely* be obtained by its use. You can cram in all the black powder the case will hold, force the bullet on top of it, crimp it any old way that holds the bullet from jumping forward and that load will go off properly and its pressures be safe. Weigh black powder, measure it, scoop it up or just fill the case and strike-off with a knife blade and you will still be safe. With all its faults it is by far the only powder for the novice to start off with and I recommend his sticking to it until the fundamentals of the reloading game have been thoroughly learned. For the chap who shoots one of those old assembled, junk-pile .45 Colts it is the one brand to stick to, because with it he can use the 250 grain lead bullet and still get about 900 feet velocity from his relic.

For most revolver cartridges, black powder should be secured in the F. F. g granulation, but for the smaller .32 cartridges the F. F. F. g will give a bit more velocity. It is peculiarly well adapted for use by the chap who cannot afford more than the very minimum in tools at the outset and who must also purchase the very lowest priced tools obtainable. Full length resizing is unnecessary, as pressures will hardly distort cases to any extent and the powder bulks up so well it always fills the case sufficiently to support the base of the bullet, so all that is necessary is to give the cartridge a good, stiff crimp.

After a "course of sprouts" with black powder, the amateur reloader will be ready to obtain a powder measure and start in on smokeless powders. By first sticking to light and then normal smokeless powder loads, checking his settings with reliable scales, he will have no trouble. I advise against the use of scoop measures with any present day smokeless powder.

With all modern smokeless powders, full length case resizing is necessary to hold the bullet friction tight and to keep it at its proper place while the crimp is being formed in the loading chamber, as well as to help prevent its receding into the case after being loaded. Never fire a smokeless powder cartridge when its bullet has receded into the case to any degree. Some smokeless powders require a certain amount of air space for proper combustion and any decrease or change in the seating depth may prove disastrous, as the pressures are sure to increase.

In closing this chapter, I am not going to pad it out with pages of lengthy tabulations of loads for the various sixguns, but prefer to insist that the reader obtain the very latest lists of such recommended charges direct from the Hercules and duPont Powder Companies. These two companies have them available for distribution at all times and are continually bringing out new and more up-to-date lists with full data on any recent developments in either cartridges or bullets. They are also constantly checking and rechecking their recommendations for pressure and velocity every time a new lot of powder is placed on the market. As they have the very finest equipment possible for such testing and experimentation, their recommendations can always be relied on and anyone adhering to the powder company lists should never run up serious pressures or encounter risk or accident if he first obtains a good working knowledge of the necessary essentials of handloading. I would particularly stress the importance of the shooter carefully checking his bullet diameter against the bore groove and cylinder throat dimensions of his guns. Also stick to the use of pistol primers in pistol cartridges, do not substitute rifle primers. If these things are carefully adhered to, any man with even a limited amount of gray matter can safely handload his sixgun ammunition.

Your stock of revolver powders should be stored in a cool and dry place, preferably where the temperature is never over 70 degrees Fahrenheit. I have had both·rifle and pistol powders dry out and become noticeably stronger after being exposed to the extreme heat of a hot, dry summer. The permissible charges then had to be cut down a grain or two, once I had to cut a heavy rifle load as much as three grains. Care should be taken that the labels pasted around the canisters do not become displaced or lost—and if such should happen see that no mistake be made when that powder is again identified and labelled. It is well to scribe the number and lot of the powder on the bottom of its canister as soon as received, then there should be no trouble in case a label comes unwrapped or is eaten off by insects.

Again, I wish to stress the necessity and importance for

beginners to adhere strictly to the powder company's loads
for a good many moons, or until the basic essentials of
handloading and ballistics are thoroughly mastered. Also
considerable knowledge should be obtained from the action
of smokeless powder, as well as some knowledge of pressure indications. Nothing is quite so safe or suitable as
black powder to start off with, but there is no necessity
of always using soft coal in your guns. No one should
attempt to handload the heavy charges I have listed or
mentioned for use with my bullets until he possesses a
thorough knowledge of all angles of the loading game,
and this knowledge should first be obtained by loading and
firing a great many normal loads. Even then, such loads
should be worked up with extreme caution, starting in
with a couple grains less powder than I advise and carefully observing all signs of pressure as the charge is carefully worked up to what I have recommended. Go slow—
about the same way a three-legged coyote would approach
a dead yearling that he had reason to believe was sur-
rounded with well concealed steel traps. If this is done,
we will have no trouble or accidents from handloading.

   We have some individuals who will read over the
powder company charges or my recommended loads, and
then say, "Well, this guy Keith used 18.5 grains of this
new #2400 powder behind his 235 grain bullet, eh?
Hell; he probably cut the charge a grain or two, in writing
about it, to make it safe for everyone, so I'll just add two
grains for a starter and get his real load." Anyone pro-
ceeding along this line of reasoning WILL get a real load—
probably a new gun also. Handloading is NOT for such
logical minded jaspers as this chap, and such have no
business shooting anything but factory loads. I once encountered a fellow who measured his charges of #5 duPont
powder by pouring them in little piles on a piece of white
paper, said he could tell by the eye just the right sized
pile of powder to make the correct charge. But he had
better eyesight than I have.

CHAPTER SEVEN

Cases for Reloading

The next thing on our list of components necessary for the reloading of revolver cartridges will be the cases. Right here will be a good place to caution against the reloading of any or all makes of recently loaded, factory cartridges which have been fired with mercuric priming. With the exception of the Remington Kleanbore, all the recent factory loadings I have fired have been primed with some such form of mercuric priming and mercury will ruin the very best cases ever made, within a few days after firing, or a few weeks time at the most. Externally, such cases may look all right, but the structure of the brass has become so rotten that in resizing the heads very often pull completely off from the body. And if there is one mean job to perform, it is to remove such a headless case from the loading chamber of a tool, generally scratching the die all up in so doing. Such rotten cases may be very dangerous to fire if reloaded, although in sizes such as .38 Special they may stand some few loadings. I recently tried to resize a bunch of fired .45 Colt Western cases in an old Ideal full length die. They stood driving into the die splendidly, but when I tried driving them out, the heads came off nearly every one, leaving the brass cylinder in the die, from which it was extremely hard to remove. I have often got as far as the crimping operation with such shells in the Pacific tool and then had the heads pull off in extracting the finished cartridge, spilling powder in the dies and causing no end of trouble.

I have finally come to the conclusion that the only fired, factory loaded cases which may be reloaded satisfactorily are the Remington Kleanbore or those Winchester cases which are primed with their non-mercuric, non-corrosive primer. I have reloaded a great many Winchester .357 Magnum cartridges and have had no trouble whatever with them, but with some other makes the heads nearly all pulled off. Therefore, if the shooter desires to buy factory ammunition and save his empties for reloading, he had better stick to the Remington Kleanbore or the Winchester with non-mercuric priming. The one best bet will be to buy new, unprimed cases from the factories and then use only straight non-mercuric, non-corrosive primers. Any make of new cases will do for reloading, if ordered unprimed and the proper primers used exclusively. When you order them, specify the uncannelured case.

The various factories use different thicknesses of brass in their cases, some being thin and some quite thick in the walls. The Western seem to be about the thickest I have used, with Winchester about the same. Remington cases run slightly thinner, but are very fine cases for the handloader and give absolute satisfaction. Most of the Peters and U. S. cases I have used seemed to be the thinnest of all, and with some makes of reloading tool they were so thin that the crimping shoulder would not form a sufficient nor an even crimp on the bullet.

Naturally there is considerable difference in the capacity of the various cases. Usually the Western and Winchester have the smallest powder capacity, as would be expected from their thick walls. This factor has quite an influence on the charge and the pressures developed, not only due to the density of loading, but also to the effect of the crimp between thick and thin cases. Naturally, the heavier the case brass, the more is the resistance necessary to force the bullet from its crimp. This difference in case thickness and powder capacity between the various makes is not generally understood and often leads to trouble. It is one reason why I dislike to recommend or list maximum loads in certain calibers. Take for instance, the .45 Auto Rim case. This caliber comes in two distinct types of case, the older style having a primer pocket protruding into the powder chamber and known as the "semi-balloon" or "folded head" type, and the modern style, developed for extreme pressures such as we encounter in the .357 Magnum where there is a heavy brass bottom or "web" to the case, the entire primer pocket being in back of this solid brass wall with its flash hole leading to the powder chamber.

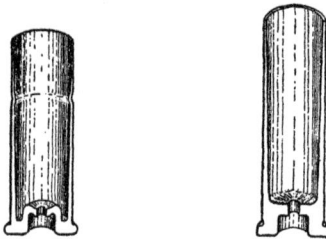

Illustrating the two distinct types of cases for modern revolver cartridges. Left sketch is a .38 Special case made with the "folding" or "semi-balloon" head, which type has been in general use for a great many years. Right sketch is a .357 Magnum case with the "solid" head, designed for withstanding extreme pressures. These terms are now in general use, but they were originally applied to an entirely different construction of center-fire, brass cartridge cases.

There is a great difference in the powder capacity between these two types of cases, and the handloader should know exactly what he is doing before reloading them. The older semi-balloon type case will hold more powder but will not withstand pressures as the more modern, heavier based case does. Furthermore, I have had both .38 and .44 Special cartridges which were reloaded a few times, blow off the entire front part of the semi-balloon pocket, finishing the case for any further use.

Most of the present day revolver cases for smokeless powder come with a cannelure scored around the body, against which rests the base of the bullet. Most of the factory loads are put up in these cannelured cases. I have never been able to figure out their reasons for this. With new cases, or cases full length resized that hold the bullet friction tight anyway, there is no real need for such a cannelure. Possibly this cannelure aids in the mechanical operations back at the factory by preventing the receding of the bullet while it is being crimped; probably it assists in waterproofing the cartridge or is an added safeguard against receding bullets, or lubricant leaking into the powder charge. I don't know however, having never been through an ammunition plant myself.

From the standpoint of the handloader, this cannelure is a damn nuisance. When such cases are fired, they invariably flatten out the ridge of metal until it becomes a mere line on the case. This in turn lengthens the fired case, when it is full length resized, to a greater length than new factory uncannelured cases. Even if not resized, this case will be of greater length than before firing, because the metal, which is flattened or forced out of that groove from the pressures of discharge, must of necessity go into increased length. Such lengthening makes it necessary to keep those cases segregated, loaded and crimped together, so that the one readjustment of the loading tool will keep the crimp in its proper place.

Light loads will not expand the cannelured case as much as will heavier loads, hence the heavier loaded, new, cannelured cases will stretch the most upon being fired. Another bad feature of the cannelured case is that if you wish to seat a bullet which is longer than the factory standard, or to seat it deeper in the case, as in some light target loads, you have trouble in getting it below that cannelure. If you force it past, the cannelure only swages down the base, making it under-size and somewhat boattailed. Either of these only further gas cutting and is no help in obtaining accuracy. Or the case bulges so it cannot be slipped into the chamber. When those cases are reloaded without full length or neck resizing, then and only then does that cannelure prove of help, as it prevents that bullet from receding in the case too deeply and crowding the powder charge. I, for one, prefer to get uncannelured cases whenever possible.

In resizing fired cases, they should always be first brushed out with a good stiff bristle, or better still a soft brass wire brush, to remove any dirt or grit from the inside. Fired cases which have been laid aside for any length of time may have a sort of gritty scale formed over the inside. This flakes off and scores the dies badly. After this brushing out they should be *slightly* oiled before resizing, and the inside of the case should also be oiled if the case mouth is going to be expanded up to a definite size after the body has been resized. A bit of practical experience is advisable here, as this oiling operation must not be overdone or the case will wrinkle in the die—just use enough very light oil to reduce friction and die wear somewhat but not enough to "feel" the oil when the case is handled. Don't get the idea that the oil may be dispensed with though, for if you have ever driven a dry case into a resizing die and then tried to get it out, you will understand what I mean.

Before oiling or being driven into the die, the cases must be *clean,* because the slightest dirt, grit or corrosion on their outsides will scar or scratch the inside of the resizing die. All these dies should be made of very hard steel, or better still, be properly hardened after manufacture, but such is not always the case, for I have to continually lap out my Pacific dies to remove slight burrs in the surface, which in turn scratches up the outside of the cases. Where this grit comes from is a mystery to me, but it always finds its way into the die in some manner or other.

The actual resizing of the fired cases may be either a comparatively easy or tough bit of work, depending upon the equipment used and the way you go about it. With the various bench tools, such as the Schmitt or the Pacific, it is not much of a job, provided the dies are kept clean and cases properly oiled. These short, pistol hulls are not nearly as hard to resize as the longer rifle cases, some of

LOADING MAGNUM POWDER CHARGES

When loading maximum or magnum charges of powder, or
any of the heavier charges recommended in this book, it is imperative that each and every charge be carefully weighed on an
accurate scale or balance. Illustration shows an ideal arrangement for such loadings. A gravity measure is used in connection
with the scale and there is nothing better than the Belding &
Mull measure shown above. Scale is the Fairbank's Miners
Assay. Each charge, as thrown from the measure, is poured onto
the scale pan and then closely trimmed to the tenth of a grain.
After which it is poured carefully into the case. Always follow
this procedure when loading Hercules Unique, No. 2400, or any
other dense powder when loaded in extreme charges. Go slow,
take your time and do the weighing accurately.

BUT, before you try any loads necessitating such close applica-
tion and care, be sure to read all of Chapter 6 of this book.

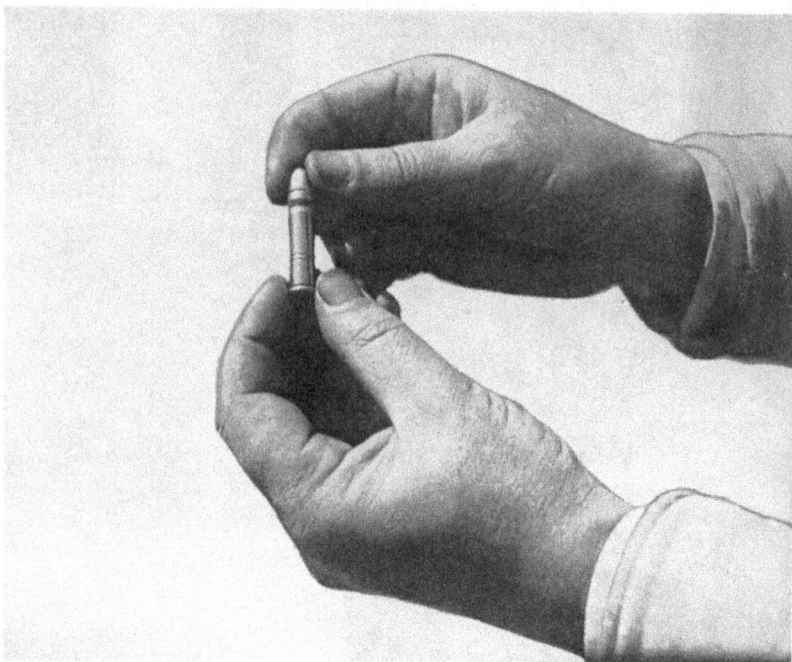

STARTING THE BULLET INTO THE CASE

In loading revolver ammunition by means of any hand tool, it is of utmost importance that each bullet be started into the case straight. No tool is necessary to perform this operation properly. Each case mouth should be flared or chamfered sufficiently to enable the bullet to enter readily without its base edge being scraped or bevelled. Then shove the bullet on in with the fingers and twist it around until its axis is parallel with that of the case and seated to a sufficient depth to hold it in that position while the assembly is being placed in the seating and crimping chamber of the tool.

which are considerable of a problem to get in and out of the dies. With most of the sixgun cartridges, the various hand resizing dies may be used with perfect satisfaction. The most important thing is to make certain the die is resting on some *solid*, substantial backing—an anvil is ideal, or a piece of heavy steel rail, even a solid stump will do. Avoid pounding cases into a die resting on a light table or bench. Use a heavy hammer for the job. Place the grain end of a short billet of hardwood against the head of the case and drive it on into the die. With the proper dies and layout you should be able to drive it clear in with one hearty "sock." In driving the case out of the die, use the correct sized drift, one large enough to barely go into the case mouth and with a recess in its base to fit over the protruding primer pocket. Do not use a smaller punch or a nail; you may only bulge out the head of the case. Most of these hand resizing dies are cheap, makeshifts anyway. I only know of one which is really fit for the job and it is not on the market. Wilson, of Cashmere, Washington, makes it on the same order as the chamber of your rifle, with the drift fitting down into the tool where it strikes against a shoulder. With this you cannot drive the case too far, neither can you batter up its head.

After being sized, the cases should be wiped dry inside, provided they have also been oiled there. Nothing is quite so good for this purpose as the proper size wooden cleaning rod with a knob type tip, on which is tied a bit of canton flannel. My reloading partner, W. L. Dickey, prefers to use fine powdered graphite on his cases instead of oil; it serves the purpose admirably but gives the cases a good black coat of graphite which does not help the appearance of the finished cartridge. It has the great advantage of doing no harm whatever inside the case, and does not have to be wiped out therefrom, as does even the slightest trace of oil.

This continued resizing of the cases is generally harder on them than the actual strain of firing, each working of the cold brass makes it more brittle until finally the case will split, usually at the neck. Some fired cases may have had a flaw in the brass or may have been fired with a mercuric primer, their next reloading causing a ruptured case. If it gets past the reloading stage, the body is apt to crack open or the head blow off when fired. Hence all such split necks or cracked body cases should be discarded the moment they are noticed.

Often, after a cartridge case has been fired and reloaded, particularly if it has been resized and the neck expanded a few times, the case will stretch, then when a bullet is crimped with the loading chamber at its normal setting, that crimp will be deeper and heavier than if the case were of standard length. This can cause high pressures, with some danger from the heavier loads. Consequently, all cases should be checked for over-all length after a few loadings and those overlength from the standard should be filed or trimmed off. There is now a splendid tool made for this purpose which every serious handloader should possess. Wilson is the maker of this case trimmer. Occasionally, new cases for the same cartridge will be found to vary in length slightly, especially different makes, and if the loading chamber is adjusted for the shorter length, it will buckle the longer case or force on it too deep and heavy a crimp.

Before reloading fired cases, always sort them out into groups of each separate make. Better still, keep them segregated and use each for the load which experience has proved best adapted to that make of case. When this is done, the differences in length, wall thickness and powder capacity will not cause trouble. Accuracy is absolutely dependent on perfect uniformity, and uniformity cannot be obtained by mixing up a batch of cases from different makes and then expecting them to hold, handle and fire the same charge with any semblance of uniformity. It would be just as logical to seat different weight bullets into our batch of cartridges and expect them to shoot into the same hole.

Cases which have been fired and reloaded many times usually become much harder than new cases, due to the working of their brass in resizing and expanding. Such cases may take or hold a heavier and stronger crimp than new brass. In time, from firing or working, these old cases usually crack at the neck and are discarded. Generally you lose a case or two every time you put the batch of empties "through the mill." Do not replace these losses' with new cases, with the view of "keeping the box full," as such a mixture of old and new brass cannot possibly give uniformity. New cases, especially those with cannelures, hold less powder, than will be the case after they have been fired a few times, flattening out that groove, and the brass wall as well, and stretching somewhat.

One feature I particularly like about new Remington cases, is the manner in which they chamfer the mouth of the case. All I have ever purchased from the factory came with the mouth carefully chamfered. They loaded slick as grease, even with the smaller Lyman tools. With the other makes, it is necessary to take a sharp knife and peel off a *slight* shaving from the inside of the mouth before loading them for the first time. On subsequent loadings, the case mouths must be expanded or flared out a mite so that the bullet can be seated without shaving off some of its base edging. As this is the steering end of the bullet, it should be kept as true as humanly possible.

If you have used black powder, the cases must be cleaned as soon as possible after firing. A can or jar of water comes in very handy on the target range. Drop the fired cases into this container as soon as ejected from the gun. Then decap and wash them out in a strong, boiling soda solution, rinse in boiling water and dry as rapidly as possible without heating them too much. Black powder residue corrodes very soon and will eat away the brass if left unchecked, completely ruining the cases for future use.

I do not particularly care about cleaning cases fired with smokeless powder, and it is seldom necessary. Cases can be cleaned perfectly with the cyanide solution recommended in Mattern's book, but there is an element of danger to it unless great care is used, and I for one do not recommend it. I have reloaded sixgun cases fired more than fifty times with smokeless powder, they were often stored for several months without any cleaning, except the brushing out and slight oiling necessary to prevent their getting so gummed up with dirt and residue that they will no longer chamber in the dies or cylinder of the gun.

Use your stock of new cases for maximum and magnum loads first, and then utilize them for a few normal loadings, gradually finishing them up for light practice charges. Finally, clean them up for the last time for "cracking down" on stuff around the house, 4th of July celebrations, etc., opportunities where misses or off shots are of no consequence. Never keep on using a case which shows a flaw in the metal or has even a slight crack at the neck, for such cracks, no matter how small, can only lead to deterioration of the powder charge in time, through permitting solvent, oil, or moisture to seep through. Even if only used for fool practice around the house that cartridge may possibly have deteriorated to such an extent that its bullet sticks in the barrel and you may ruin the gun on the next shot.

CHAPTER EIGHT

Primers and Priming

The modern small-arms primer is such an ordinary look-ing bit of apparatus and can be put into place so readily with simple tools, that the average handloader is apt to get a bit careless when it comes to the easy but important opera-tion of repriming. As a matter of fact, in my early days, I knocked out many a fired primer with a small nail and then shoved the new one in place with a home made punch. Strange to say, these primers all worked nicely, after a fashion, but then they generally do this anyhow. To me, one of the mysteries of this present day, is how the primer will stand the abuse and misuse commonly given it and not go off prematurely, yet pop so surely every time the firing pin strikes it.

There is a great deal more to this vital operation of repriming than appears at the surface or is to be found printed on the box in which they are packed. First off, *use pistol primers* in pistol cartridges. While it is true that rifle primers of the same size may be substituted, in some cases with apparent satisfaction, the practice is to be con-demned. Primers for use in the larger capacity rifle car-tridges are apt to be made of different metal and to contain a much stronger pellet. These are intended to "spit" a more intense flame, one sufficient to ignite the larger grained, tubular, dense powders, and to withstand extremely high pressures without piercing or flowing back around the firing pin. Generally speaking, it takes a much heavier hammer blow and different "percussion" to detonate a rifle primer.

They may not respond quickly enough if loaded into revolver cases and those cartridges used in speed firing, also
the pressures developed may be too great.

Then, it is much the best to use the pistol primer of the
same make as the cases being loaded; in other words, follow
the manufacturer's advice, and when using his cases, prime
them with the primer he made and intended to be used in
the distinctive primer pocket which may be formed only in
his make of cartridge. There may be slight, but appreciable differences between the various makers' product of the
same case. I have found some in which the inner edge of
the primer pocket was rounded, while in others, it ran out
to a square edge. The primer intended for use in the
former pocket had a rounded front edge and if inserted
into the square edged pocket of the latter would seat too
deeply, possibly having to be "squashed" a mite to grip
properly. This compression does not do the pellet a bit of
good either. Furthermore, some makes of primer are designed with a convex or fully rounded face, while others
are appreciably flattened on this outer surface; the protrusion of your hammer nose may not be quite sufficient to
reach the latter type if loaded into the wrong cases.

While it is true the average handloader indulges in rather
indiscriminate substitution in this matter of using one
maker's primer in another make of case, and with apparent
satisfaction in most instances, the practice is not to be recommended. Best results, by far, will always be obtained
by using W. R. A. primers in Winchester cases, and so on.

The principle of repriming the fired case is extremely
simple. The new primer should be inserted *squarely* into
the pocket and pushed home until it bears solidly against
the bottom wall (or "web") of the powder chamber. There
must be no lost motion or play by the primer when struck
by the firing pin, detonation should be instantaneous, and
the full flame from the priming compound should "spit"
through the flash hole into the powder charge. In perform-
ing this exceedingly simple operation, the greatest of care

must be observed to avoid disturbing the priming compound, or "pellet" as some call it. This composition should
not be mashed, pulverized or displaced in the least. This
being pretty apt to occur if the primer is shoved in cock-
eyed, or flattened too much in an attempt to make certain
it is properly bearing against the web of the case.

Evidently, some of our loading tool manufacturers treat
priming as if it were a sort of by-pass to more essential
operations, and have arranged their tool accordingly. Take
the old Ideal tong tools for example—these come equipped
with the early "nut cracker" type of priming arrangement,
where the primer is squeezed into the case by hand pressure,
with no method of guidance or stop gauge to indicate when
seated enough. This worked very well with black powder,
for which the tool was designed, as this old soft-coal only
needs the suggestion of a flame to start it off right. The
main thing to remember in priming with these tong tools is
to start the primer in squarely, and to stop the pressure in
time and not flatten the cup or pulverize the compound.
When a primer slips in easily, there is a tendency to mash
it out a bit so it will "fit" better. In any event, it is hard
to properly gauge this seating operation by the "feel," which
we are obliged to do with this type of tool. A much better
method is to knock off that useless bullet push-rod intended
for sizing, then insert a suitable stop gauge (made in tee or
rivet shape) into the allegedly round sizing die. With a
bit of experimenting, this stop-gauge can be filed down
until the handles can be closed only the exact amount necessary to properly seat the primer. Another point is that it
finally lets the owner make some good use of that fool
sizing hole. This stunt permits very accurate seating of the
primers with these tong tools, but it remains a hard matter
to start some of them into the pocket squarely as they will
smash sideways or become badly distorted; still, the smaller
sized pistol primers work very well with some calibers and
makes of cases.

Another trouble often encountered is that the primer

seating punch may not be ground down smoothly or to
proper contour, or it may be off-center in some tools. I
have owned many old Ideal tools in which the seating
punch would mar and distort the primer, often leaving
lines scored across it which could not help but favor the
piercing of the primer if pressures got a bit high. Right
now, we have one Pacific primer punch which was drilled
out too deeply or with too much of a taper to its center;
this punch leaves the seated primer with a raised teat
in its center that is bound to rub across the recoil shield
of a sixgun and it is impossible to seat the primers below
the level of the base of a case with it. Needless to say,
this punch is going back to Pacific P.D.Q. Any deformation of the primer such as this is very apt to break up
and powder the "pellet" of priming mixture inside the
cup—being then in a powdered form instead of the hard
cake intended, it cannot offer the proper resistance between
the cup and anvil necessary for instant and uniform detonation. Do not put up with *any* distortion or marking
of the primer cup with *any* make of tool.

The Ideal #2 Re-and Decapping tool is a much better
arrangement for priming, and when you get hold of one
properly assembled and adjusted (not all of them are),
you have a pretty accurate hand tool, about as good as
could be desired. With this #2 tool, the primer can be
dropped into the carriage, all slack taken up and the case
then given a twirl with the fingers which will automatically
square-up the primer and start it into the pocket accurately.
Then, if the seating punch was adjusted correctly at the
factory (which it may not be) that primer will be seated
to exactly the correct depth until it bears properly against
the web, by which time the handle is past dead-center and
you cannot smash or distort the pellet in the least. Occasionally, I have purchased one in which everything clicked
just right, it is a most pleasing, efficient and rapid tool to
use when so properly adjusted. To be really worthwhile,
there should be some method by which the seating punch

can be reversed—one end used for round-faced primers and the other for flat ones. The middle of this seating punch also should be threaded, so it may be accurately adjusted for seating depth.

Some of the larger hand and bench tools come equipped with a priming arrangement which is entirely O.K. The Belding & Mull is an exceptionally good one when properly adjusted. The Schmitt and Pacific are also good, and perform the de- and recapping of the case along with other operations, permitting good time to be made, yet doing precision work also.

In seating, it is imperative that the primer be forced slightly below the base of the case and not left flush or protruding. Any protruding primer is dangerous, whether fired in rifle or sixgun; such is also the cause of an occasional misfire. It may project so far out of the case as to rub across the recoil shield of the gun and fire prematurely or else put undue stress on the hand which revolves the cylinder, which at times may tie up the arm.

When priming with the hand tools, it is a good idea to place each primed case mouth down into a suitable loading block. When finished, pick up this filled loading block, hold it about level with the eyes with the cases all slanting one way, then cock your shooting eye across those bases and make certain every primer is seated slightly *below* the level of the base. With a little practice, any protruding primer will be instantly spotted by this method. In my opinion, this check-up is almost as necessary as the same operation performed later on at the other end of the case with a view of detecting double powder charges.

Misfires seldom happen if even ordinary care is taken in the priming operation, but can occur, however, from a protruding primer, as the hammer blow may merely seat it deeper in the case pocket and yet not mash the pellet; they can also occur through the primer cup being mashed so badly in insertion that its detonating compound is pulverized and displaced out from between the cup and its anvil. For certain, instantaneous operation, the primer depends upon this pellet being undisturbed until it is mashed between the primer cup and anvil by the indentation of the hammer-blow. See that your priming operations and handling are conducted in accordance with these principles.

The stability of small-arms primers is amazing. I have often loaded some whose age I knew to be around twenty-five years, yet they functioned perfectly when fired. The

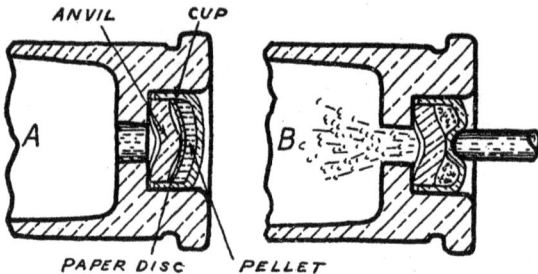

Illustrating the correct principles of priming and ignition. Sketch A shows primer properly seated in case pocket—anvil bearing firmly against web, with cup seated squarely and below base of case, pellet undisturbed. B shows action at instant firing pin strikes—note that the anvil takes up the shock of hammer blow and that detonation is effected by mashing pellet between anvil and cup.

past few years have seen the primer situation somewhat upset by the introduction of all these various non-corrosive, non-mercuric, non-skid types of primer composition, some of which were not yet out of the experimental stage when put on the market. A few have proven to be reliable and somewhat in keeping with the claims made by their manufacturers, while several others have not. I would strongly advise using only the Remington and Winchester, non-mercuric and non-corrosive types, or the Frankford Arsenal non-mercuric; all of which have proved dependable for me.

There are two sizes of primers manufactured for revolver cartridges, and in some few calibers it is possible to obtain cases made for either. The larger sized primer is usually the more powerful. The powder charge which is maximum for the case with the smaller primer may prove a little on the danger side if loaded into a case taking the larger one. Follow the recommendations very closely in such matters, or else cut the charge a trifle and again work up slowly to the full load in instances where the large-primer case must be used.

Occasionally one hears of handloaders who consider it necessary to ream out the flash hole of the case to a larger diameter. This is unnecessary and dangerous in the extreme. The manufacturers have already made that flash hole as large as necessary with due regard to the danger of back pressure from the charge. Let it alone. If it were possible to safely have it any larger, they would have made it so. Each manufacturer has his own ideas as to just what diameter this flash hole should be—when used with HIS primer; another argument for using only that primer in his case.

Expelling the fired primer, or decapping, as it is commonly called, is an operation which is not likely to cause trouble if the right tool is used and the old primer has not been permitted to corrode in the case pocket. The various bench type tools generally do this along with one or two other operations, so it is not much of a problem with them. With some makes of tool their decapping pin bushing will be found to be much smaller than the inside diameter of the case, especially with the Belding & Mull; this is considerable of a nuisance as one must fish about for the flash hole with the point of the decapping pin, then when located, insert the pin on into the flash hole and hold it there until the pressure of the hand lever takes up all slack and punches the old primer out. All decapping pin bushings should be made almost the full inside diameter of the case neck for accurate centering and prompt and convenient expulsion of the fired primer—but some are not.

Generally, it pays to expel the primer from the case

pocket shortly after the cartridge is fired, do not allow your empty cases to stand around until those old, fired primers have become corroded. At times, where cases are apt to be laid aside for several months before being used again, it is advisable to do this single operation by itself. This is a job to which almost any old cow poke who drops in for the day can be safely put at—he is not apt to do much harm other than break off a decapping pin or two, and any experienced handloader will have a plentiful supply of these extra pins on hand anyhow.

CHAPTER NINE

Reloading Operations

Having assembled all our necessary components and discussed their adaptability, merits and shortcoming, let us now take up, step by step, the reloading of a cartridge. If new, primed cases will be used, they must first be lightly chamfered at the mouth (unless of Remington make) and then belled slightly. Years ago, the Smith & Wesson outfit used to furnish a special tool for this purpose, made on the order of a straight-line bullet seater. This was well worth its cost and the trouble of that extra operation. If present day bench tools are used, they come equipped to perform this operation; if not, then it must be done by hand. Be careful not to chamfer or flare out the mouth of the case to too great an extent.

If fired cases are to be reloaded, they must first be decapped. With the Schmitt, Pacific and similar large bench tools this is a simple operation, they not only decap but also reprime the case, as well as full length resize and expand the inside of its neck to a uniform diameter—all in one simple operation and with one stroke of the lever. Care should be taken to see that the dies are carefully adjusted so that the cases will be properly belled at the mouth and the new primer seated completely into the pocket with its face just below the level of the case head. These two mentioned tools are equipped with an automatic primer feed, the primers first being loaded into a magazine. One should see that they are all turned the same way and loaded into the primer charger in the position which seats them anvil down into the case pocket.

117

With the combination type of hand tools the primer must first be started into the pocket with the fingers and then forced in place, gently but firmly, until fully seated. I much prefer to use the Ideal #2 tool for this purpose, because it does the two operations of decapping and re-priming at one handling, and if properly adjusted at the factory, will prime the case very accurately and satisfactorily. Any tool or seating punch which distorts the primer, mars its face or smashes it in the least should be discarded, as it does not further accuracy to have the priming compound broken or displaced.

I am greatly in favor of using the more expensive, heavier bench types of reloading tools. It is true they cost much more, but in the long run they prove to be the least expensive and are far more satisfactory. With most of the hand tools, it takes so many more operations to put an empty, fired case in shape to reload. If your time is worth anything, it is much the best to purchase the heavier, speedier bench tools which will accomplish several of these necessary operations with one motion of the operating lever. Not only will they do these operations in much less time, they are capable of greater precision with closer adjustment, and the work is done with far less effort on the part of the operator.

The greatest weakness of the hand tool becomes apparent in full-length resizing of the fired case, or even in neck resizing with some cartridges. In many instances, the case may be reloaded and fired several times, in close chambered guns, without this full-length resizing, but by far the best results will be obtained if this operation is always performed. I know of no tong type of tool which will do even neck resizing with ease or accuracy, although this operation is comparatively easy with the bench tools. When it comes to full-length resizing of the fired case, the heavy bench tool is in its element. To do this operation with a hand resizing die, the latter must be placed on a heavy, solid foundation, then the oiled case is started into the resizing chamber and a section of hardwood used as a drift. Strike the drift a direct blow with a heavy hammer or mallet until the case is driven entirely in with its head flush or rim against the face of the die. The operation should be performed with a minimum of hammering, accomplish it with as few blows as possible so the case will not become expanded before it enters the die; with the proper layout and skill most revolver cartridges can be driven in with one good tap. I have found that a heavy hammer works better than a mallet for such work, as one hits more nearly center and in line with it than with the bigger mallet. Always drive the case out of the die with the proper punch usually provided with the tool. Where the case must be resized with hand tools, the operation is best done first, before decapping and repriming.

After this resizing operation, the case will usually be too small at the mouth to allow the bullet to enter properly, so must be slightly belled. Some tools have made provision for this operation by providing an expanding plug, such as the lower end of the loading chamber on the Lyman, or the rod end of the Belding & Mull. With such tools, care must be taken to bell the case mouth but slightly, just enough to permit the bullet to enter and no more, because excessive flaring may split or prevent it from entering the loading chamber.

The smaller hand tools, such as the Lyman, B. & M. or Bond, will resize only the neck of the case. Examine such resized cases carefully and make certain that the die and operation leaves the neck in perfect alignment with the body of the case; I have seen many which would not do so. If the tool neck-resizes one side of the case more than the other, discard or return it to the factory, for accurate ammunition cannot be turned out from such a tool.

The combination of components you have selected may not be entirely suited to the dimensions of the hand tools being used, and it may be necessary to expand the inside of the neck after the case had been resized. Cases vary in thickness, you know, and an extra thick case will mean greater restriction, with consequent less inside diameter at the neck, than those made of thinner brass. This, in turn, means more bullet pull and can cause a variation in pressure which is not conducive to accuracy, or even safety for that matter. In fact, with some heavy cases the inside neck diameter may be such that the bullet cannot be seated without distortion. The Belding & Mull hand tool expands the neck of the case to uniform inside diameter, as all tools should do. This operation is often another argument for the much better bench tools.

I believe all fired cases should at least be neck resized before being again reloaded, but better results will be obtained under almost all conditions if they are full length resized and the inside of the neck then expanded to the proper uniform diameter.

After the fired case has been reworked into proper shape, we come to the powder charging. This is a relatively simple, yet important operation, upon which much depends and from which serious trouble may occur if done improperly. For all light to normal charges, there is nothing quite so handy or safe as the Lyman, B. & M. or similar gravity powder measures, used in conjunction with an accurate scale or balance and kept in necessary working order by frequent inspection and cleaning. An accurate scale, weighing to one-tenth grain is necessary to check up any powder measure—and they should be checked frequently. Before setting the measure for the charge desired, go over it carefully and clean it up a bit, making sure that there are no dirt or cobwebs in the drop tube which might hold up part of a charge. See to it that this tube is seated fully up into its socket and securely clamped. No parts should be gummed up or oily. Once the proper setting is obtained, the locking nut or set screw should be turned up tightly enough to hold the setting against any possibility of movement, yet not so tight as to strip the threads.

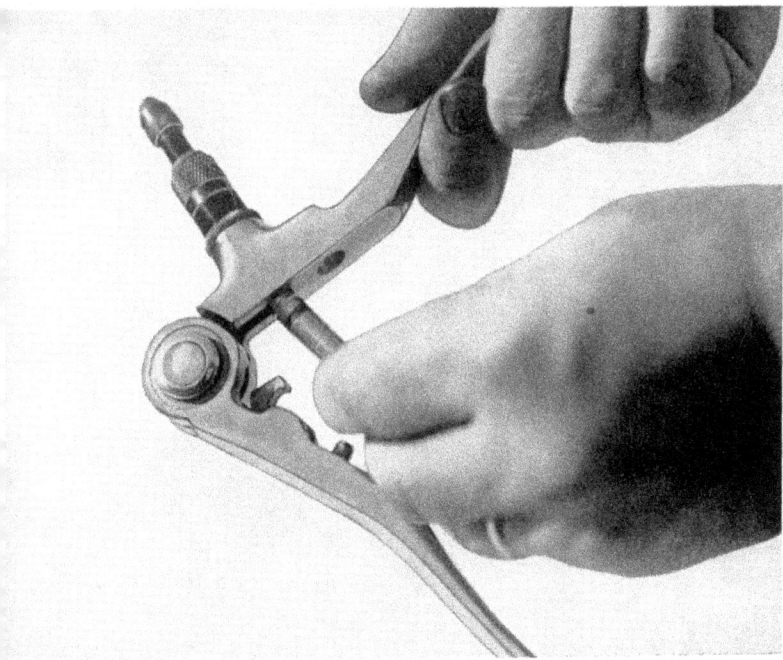

FORMING THE CARTRIDGE

The assembled components are shown being inserted into the loading chamber of the tool in order to complete seating of the bullet and the crimping of the case.

There is a knack to doing this properly. The tool should be held so the case is inserted with bullet pointing upwards, to avoid its falling out. Shove the case on into the chamber as far as it will readily go and then give its base a twirl with the fingers to assist in further aligning the bullet accurately. Then bring the handles together and turn the tool over to complete the crimping operation.

Make certain there is no grease or dirt on the point of the bullet before it is inserted into the loading chamber. Do not permit the latter to become clogged up with any foreign matter which might result in the improper seating of the bullet.

CRIMPING THE CARTRIDGE

Revolver cartridges should be crimped heavily; a strong crimp resistance being necessary to burn the powder charge properly.

In using hand tools, form this crimp with a slow and steady pressure until the tool handles will close no further. Go easy about this final operation and if any cartridge offers unusual resistance or the tool seems to jam, stop and see what is wrong. A buckled case will undoubtedly result in a clogged loading chamber, necessitating the dismounting of the tool and a consequent readjustment of all parts; which can only mean a loss of time—and a few spoiled cartridges.

Make periodic checks with the scales to see that the setting remains undisturbed.

The hopper should be kept at least half full of powder at all times. Leave the cover off in order to see that it does not run too low. The Belding & Mull is supposed to be the exception to this rule, as it has a charging chamber separate from the big hopper; however, I prefer to keep even this measure over half full, although it will throw accurate charges as long as the lower, glassed-in compartment is filled with powder. With this B. & M., which is known as the visible powder measure, owing to the glass front over its lower reservoir, the charge drops into a small tube and is then cut off exactly and uniformly at each throw of the operating lever. The charge must then be poured, by means of a funnel, into the cases. This measure is claimed to be the most accurate of all, but in actual operation it is much slower than the Ideal and other similar measures; also, this additional operation of pouring the charge from the tube through the funnel offers an opportunity of spilling a few grains now and then. In using the Ideal measure, the empty case is held under the mouth of the drop tube and the charge thrown directly into it. Various sized tubes may be obtained for all calibers. An up-and-down stroke is made with the operating lever, then the little knocker at the side is given a flip with the forefinger to jar out all the powder and the job is done. If the drop tube is kept clean and tightly clamped in place and the operations done uniformly, this is a very accurate and reliable powder measure, and is the one I prefer for loading revolver cartridges where light or normal loads are used.

For magnum or hand weighed loads, I like the Belding & Mull measure, as it can be set just under the charge wanted, this allowing the under-charge to be thrown on the scale pan, where one can then add the necessary few grains to balance. An empty case can be used in a similar manner with the Ideal measure, it really works about as

well, except for the fact that you do not have as convenient
a tube to hold in the hand. However, a most satisfactory
sort of tube may readily be improvised from some of the
larger caliber, straight rifle cases.

The powder charge for maximum loads should *always*
be weighed out, not thrown from these gravity measures.
If you do not happen to own an accurate balance, assay
or gold scale, borrow one from some friend—or cut down
the load if you cannot get it. Use the friend's scale to
check measure settings also, and while over there for this
purpose you had better accurately mark the setting with
a scribe, then it can be kept to that mark. All the various
measure manufacturers print tables in their catalog showing the settings of the measure slides, but such are only
approximate. These measures should never be used for
normal or heavy charges of smokeless powder unless
checked by means of accurate scales and then closely
watched and kept at that setting. With black powder, these
tables and slide settings can be used safely, but with all
smokeless powders I advise a close check with the scales
and then a periodic "check and double check."

The charging of cases should always be done in conjunction with a loading block, which may be purchased
from any tool maker or easily made by the shooter. It pays
to have on hand several of these blocks, of thickness and
size suitable to the various caliber cartridges being loaded
—the holes should be sufficiently large to take the head
of the case without crowding and deep enough to hold
the case securely, yet permit it to be gripped with the
fingers when removing. Make them to take 50 or even
100 cases, large enough not to be tipped over.

After the charges have all been thrown and charged
cases placed in the loading block, it is a wise precaution
to take the block to where the light is good and there go
over every case with the eye and make certain none has
received a double charge. *Do not neglect this precaution
when using the denser smokeless powders such as Bullseye*

or #5. Some powders, such as #80 or #2400, bulk up so well that it would be very hard, if not impossible, to throw two charges into the same case, while with some of the condensed powders such as Bullseye, this would not be noticeable unless closely scrutinized.

When loading black powder into some of the heavier walled cases it may be a hard matter to get the charge in without unduly crushing it in seating the bullet. The answer to this (and similar problems with smokeless powders) is to pour the charge slowly into the case through a long tube and allow each grain to settle properly, which it cannot do if dumped rapidly into a funnel. The Lyman outfit sell these long tubes for such purposes. By using one and turning the crank slowly, the charge will have time to settle much better than any amount of jarring and thumping. In loading some of the larger black powder, rifle cartridges, I have often been obliged to use a long tube and then tap the case considerably while pressing a length of steel rod on top of the charge.

Charging the cases is an operation best performed while alone; if a friend or assistant should be around all hands must attend strictly to their own business while the charges are being thrown. The person operating the powder measure should attain a regular cadence and sequence *and keep his mind on the job.* Do it "by the numbers" as they say in the Army. Both the measuring or weighing of powder charges should be done with the greatest of care and attention to details, with no careless or slipshod methods allowed. The better the equipment used for this operation, the nearer perfect the results, and the more satisfactory will be the finished ammunition. Personally, I prefer to use the double block system, keeping to my left one block in which are the primed cases, mouth down as they were positioned when inspected for protruding primers. I take out one of these empty cases with my left hand, charge it properly and accurately, and then place it mouth up into another block placed to my right—*and I don't like to be bothered while shifting these cases around, either.*

Now that we have the cases correctly charged with powder, our next step will be to adjust the loading tool properly in order to accurately seat and crimp the bullet. All loading chambers should be double adjustable, that is, adjustable for case length, and the degree of crimp given, and also adjustable for bullet seating depth, so as to seat the bullet and crimp it exactly where desired. With such a chamber, the tool may be adjusted to crimp or not, as desired. Any tools which do not provide adjustments such as these should be discarded, as they will not permit the proper assembly of various makes of components or allow any variation whatsoever in the bullet used.

When adjusting any tool for a new cartridge or combination of components, it is best to first slightly unscrew the case length and crimp adjustment. Then take an empty case, similar to those being used and, placing it in the loading chamber, so adjust the length of crimp that the case will not go completely into the die, but will project out about a thirty-second of an inch—that is, it should lack that much of seating flush into the die. If plenty of old cases are on hand, especially some old mercuric primer cases, they can be utilized for such adjustments; in fact, it pays to keep a supply on hand for just this purpose. Once the crimp adjustment is correct, clamp it up tightly with the set collar provided. It has been my experience that the one set collar with which the tong type tools are provided is not enough for the purpose. It pays to obtain an extra supply of these collars so that you can fit two to every loading chamber and bullet seating punch. Once the correct adjustment is obtained and these two collars set up tightly, that adjustment stays correct.

Next comes the adjustment for bullet seating depth. Take the bullet seating screw, or punch, and screw it back until it is well out from its proper adjustment. Place a bullet in the mouth of the case, insert it in the chamber and close the tool until you feel the first sign of pressure, then remove and examine for position of bullet. Adjust accordingly and repeat this operation until the bullet is seated correctly and with a suitable crimp forming in its crimping groove. Here is where a few more old mercuric primed cases can be used. Load them up as dummies and keep a supply around for speedy and accurate use as tool adjusting gauges. Adjust your tool so that it will form an accurate and heavy crimp in the crimp groove, yet not so heavy that it will crush or distort the case any.

After the tool is properly adjusted, with its lock screws or collars turned up tightly so that they will stay that way, take your primed and powder charged case and start the base of the bullet into the case mouth with the fingers, assuming of course, that you have cleaned all traces of grease or lubricant from the bullet base. Align that bullet as correctly as you can with the axis of the cartridge, and seat it sufficiently to stay that way while it is being inserted in the tool. Slip it into the loading chamber and repeat the seating and crimping operation. Examine the first few cartridges closely for crimp adjustment, for a too heavy or improperly positioned crimp may bulge the case just in back of its mouth. Once the tool is properly adjusted and securely clamped, there should be no further trouble as long as the same make of cases are used, and no difficulty should be experienced in completing the loading of that batch of ammunition.

The charged cases, with bullet seated in their mouths, should always be inserted upwards into the loading chamber of the tong type tools to avoid any possibility of a spill. Any surplus grease should be removed from the bullet points in order to prevent the front of the loading chamber from becoming gummed up with it and seating improperly. To the uninitiated, it might seem that the tool has changed its adjustment, whereas it really needs to be cleaned out. If the loading chamber should become gummed up with surplus lubricant, stop and remove all such dirt with a cloth on the end of a small stick.

In seating the bullets and crimping the case on them do so slowly and with a minimum of effort. Do not try to force things, if it should require undue exertion to form the crimp on a certain cartridge, you better stop and see what is wrong. Nothing is more troublesome or exasperating than to buckle a case in the loading chamber. This generally calls for the complete dismounting of the tool in order to remove the cartridge and a consequent complete readjustment of everything. There are times when an extra long cartridge can cause an unbelievable amount of trouble in tying up the loading tool.

Certain sixgun cartridges may be particularly hard to reload at times. I refer to the .32/20, .38/40 and .44/40. For some reason or other, these three calibers seem to be made of thinner brass than the other sizes, and often when one comes to putting a crimp on the cartridge, their bottle-necked construction causes the case walls to collapse easily. With some lots of cases or type of bullet it is practically impossible to do a proper job, as so many cases will buckle-up in the loading chamber of the tool. It is often the usual thing to lose six or seven cases out of each lot being reloaded. I had a lot of this trouble in loading for my .38/40 and it was one of the reasons why I went to the straight .45 Colt case. At times, the trouble may be remedied by making two or three operations out of the bullet seating and crimping: screw out the loading chamber so the tool will not crimp, run the lot of cartridges through the tool and seat the bullets properly, but do not put any crimp whatever on the case. Then adjust for crimp only, make another run through and crimp the cartridges. It may be necessary to make two distinct operations of this crimp, setting the tool for a light crimp first time and then increasing this crimp on a second attempt. There can be combinations with which it is almost, if not actually impossible, to turn out a satisfactory job with one of these calibers.

It may be well here to say a few words about the different types of bullet seaters and loading chambers. For loading metal cased bullets in rifle cartridges, the straight line "die-and-plunger" sets like the Niedner, Dubiel, Belding & Mull are very fine tools, and will do a perfectly satisfactory job *when properly made*. Notice I say "when properly made"; very few of them are. Much talk about "precision", "accuracy", "close dimensions" etc. is heard from the various makers of these tools, yet the sad fact is that most of them are made to about as close tolerances as are used by the tinsmiths in turning out rain-spouts. To be worth some of the prices paid and to give satisfaction to the user, any precision, straight line bullet seater should be made to about the dimensions of a maximum rifle chamber, with the lands reamed out of an oversized bore, this specification will come about as close to what is required as anything I can think of. The "bore" of the tool should fit the bullet so closely that it can be seated down into the neck of the case without its base edge *touching* the mouth of the case, assuming that there is a slight chamfer to the latter, which there should be. Any bullet, loaded in a tool properly made as I have described, will be truly seated in a "straight line", and what is more important its base will remain as perfect as it was when it left the factory, not having a segment of the base edge scraped off by one side of the case mouth.

Exceedingly few of the commercial tools will do this. I have a friend who recently received a .25 Niedner Krag, and with it he bought a "precision" bullet seating "die". Its maker demonstrated Dutch economy by making the tool from the left-over end of the rifle barrel; by the time he had reamed out all lands sufficiently and polished up the tool its bore measured an exact .263″ instead of the .258″ specified. The only thing right about this tool was its price.

However, whether properly made or not, I do not like

this type of bullet seating chamber in the least for loading revolver cartridges for the following reasons: The
case is placed in the chamber of the die and the latter
fitted into the safety base in order to prevent any metal
coming in contact with the primer while the bullet is
being seated. Then the bullet is dropped down the bore
of the die, and "dropped" is right, because it invariably
falls down until it strikes the mouth of the case, whereas
it should be necessary, with a properly made tool, to shove
it lightly down by hand with almost enough pressure to
amount to what a machinist would term a "push" fit—
at any rate the bullet should fit closely to the bore of the
die, which it seldom does with the average specimen of
straight line tool. Upon dropping the bullet in, the
seating plunger is slipped on top of it, after which there
is struck a sharp blow on the top of the plunger to seat
the bullet to its proper depth, and also to form the crimp
with some tools. These latter tools do not permit any
adjustment to form the proper degree of crimp or to allow
for slight differences in length which may exist between
different lots of cases.

Also, and worst of all, unless very closely chambered
(which most are not as I have said before), this blow of
the mallet necessary to seat the bullet or form the crimp
is pretty apt to have some upsetting effect upon a soft,
lead revolver bullet. At times, this upsets the larger calibered bullets until they are no longer of correct diameter
for the gun they are to be fired in. I may be wrong in
this contention, but from my experience and from my
findings in the case of one .45 Colt gun blown up with
this type of loading tool used, I believe that revolver
bullets should be seated and the cartridge crimped with
a steady, even push or pressure and not by any blow from
a hammer or mallet. There is too great a tendency for
that soft bullet to upset, or "slug up" as the ballisticians
express it.

Many years ago, I learned in loading muzzle loading

rifles—both the old heavy-slug muzzle loaders and the Pope, Schoyen, Petersen and Ballard breech-muzzle loaders —that in order to properly seat the bullet down through the false-muzzle, it must be done with *one* sharp, heavy blow struck with the palm of the hand. If several successive, light blows were struck, that bullet would be greatly upset, and as a result was then hard to push on down with the loading rod to its proper seating depth ahead of the chamber. It is obvious that no one strikes as hard a blow with the palm of his hand to these bullet starters as is applied with a mallet when seating a revolver bullet into a case having its neck resized to hold that bullet friction tight, and then to form a deep and uniform crimp in a heavy and stiff brass case. To me, the principle is all wrong and I consider it highly dangerous if used with cartridges developing maximum or magnum ballistics; I may be wrong in this contention but I shall stick to it until I am shown otherwise.

For metal patched rifle loads, such bullet seaters are very fine indeed, but then these loads are seldom crimped. Also the hard metal patch bullet resists such deformation and upsettage much better than the relatively soft, lead revolver bullet. For seating the .32/20, .38/40 and .44/40 metal patched bullets for use in revolver cartridges, this type of bullet seater will prove to be all right, but I do not favor it for seating or crimping any soft lead bullet.

Some of the loading tool makers are rather careless about a few thousandths of an inch in the tolerances of their tools and dies. It is best for the purchaser to specify exactly what he wants in the thousandths of an inch when it comes to bullet sizing dies. Then it would be well when they are received to size down a few bullets and take a micrometer and make certain that they will do the work as specified, checking not only for diameter across one way, but also go all around that sized bullet, and make certain it is true. If it comes from the die with one reading greater than the other and is obviously out of round, or its diameter is different from that ordered, send it back for correction. Make certain that you know how to handle the micrometer first, because not everyone can do this properly.

Another fault to watch out for in some makes of tools, in fact the Schmitt is the only tool in which I have not encountered this trouble at times, is having too large a diameter in the loading chamber or sizing dies. This fault can generally be seen at a glance, as the finished cartridge will come from the chamber with a well-formed crimp on one side and only a slight one on the other. This trouble may also be caused by having cases which are too thin walled. If the chamber will not form a perfect crimp with at least one make of case, send it back to its maker for correction. This will mean a new loading chamber. As I have previously stated, different makes of cases vary greatly in thickness, and where some one make may be too thin to form a proper crimp in your tool, another make of the same case may work perfectly. The ammunition companies are improving their product all the time and with the recent two consolidations of the various smaller companies, we can look for an even greater improvement and standardization in the immediate future. As a result of these consolidations, this thin case business will soon be a thing of the past.

Some oversize loading chambers will often seat and crimp a bullet out of line with the axis of its case. Such improperly seated bullets cannot shoot accurately in the finest gun ever made. This may occur with the tong and hand tools or even with the straight line, custom made bullet seaters if the latter are not made to proper close tolerances. All seating or loading dies, whether for rifle or revolver cartridges, must hold the bullet in a straight line with the axis of the case before the bullet seating plunger is forced home, otherwise the bullet will be started into the case out of line, its base and sides will be shaved in places and it is very likely to be crimped tightly in that crooked position, whereupon the fault can no longer be seen with the naked eye and there you have one cartridge which cannot possibly shoot accurately.

The better and more complete your loading equipment, the better and safer will be the cartridges you produce, provided that the old bean is also used in their production. Regardless of how well a reloading tool is made, it cannot perform its operations properly unless some gray matter is also used in the handling of this tool. Most of the revolver charges recommended in the Ideal and other hand books are safe, conservative loads and are listed there for that very good reason. The beginner, therefore, will do well to stick to such loads until he has acquired plenty of actual, practical experience with them, then he may safely venture a bit further and use more powerful charges. Do not try to assemble maximum or magnum loads with no equipment other than a cheap, combination, hand or tong type tool, it takes a proper assortment of adjustable, precision tools and their accessories to tackle such loads with safety and confidence.

I have never used a finer precision tool than the Schmitt, while the Pacific is a very close second. The Pacific at times is slightly faster than the Schmitt as the loaded cases are inserted mouth up into its loading die, to seat and crimp the bullet. This facilitates handling without danger of spilling the powder. Still, the Schmitt has certain advantages not possessed by the other; the bullet can be started in the case with the fingers, case set down on the workbench and the die placed over it, whereupon the assembly is held friction tight and then placed in the tool and its lever operated. No tool will produce finer ammunition than the Schmitt, but the Pacific is very good also and as I have said before, it is the faster of the two. For rifles loads, I prefer the Schmitt, principally on account of greater power and more certain seating of heavy rifle bullets and primers, and the extreme precision of the chambering of its dies necessary for such work.

I have had no experience with the more elaborate automatic type of bench reloading machine suitable for military and police organizations or the larger clubs. These tools are very costly and the men who operate them are generally old shooters and experienced reloaders—men who do not need to be told what to do or how to do it. Such tools do the complete reloading operation with a minimum of adjustment and operation; in fact, they are miniature factory loading machines, and are far beyond the reach of the average shooter. I have used the Lyman, and the older Ideal tools for a great many years, and although much has been said against this type of tong tool, when they are properly handled they will produce splendid ammunition and very good results may be secured with them. Also, they are small, light, easily moved about, and they do not break a man up by their cost. But I strongly believe in buying the Schmitt or Pacific tools in every case where the handloader can afford them, particularly if his time is valuable, as they will do so many operations at one stroke of the operating lever that a great deal more ammunition can be loaded in the same time than with the cheaper type of hand tool.

The finally loaded cartridges should always be wiped clean of all excess dirt and lubricant and carefully packed in proper boxes. Those boxes had best be labeled as to the primer, powder charge, bullet weight, shape and temper used. The date of loading is also advisable. A good plan is to have a quantity of gummed labels made up in the form of a pad, having these details printed thereon and blank spaces left to be properly filled in for each load. Space for bullet diameter can also be useful. It is well to keep a record of all loadings, their performances, accuracy, pressure indications, etc. for future reference, otherwise your reloads will soon become so badly mixed up, that it will be impossible to tell which is which or for what is which. It does not pay to have too great a variety of small lots of cartridges lying about. Often it is well to adopt some distinguishing mark for the nose of the bullet; then if you travel about with a cartridge belt filled with both grouse and big game reloads, you can distinguish the one from the other at a glance—possibly at a touch also. However; I am not recommending that this be done, I just suggest the stunt in case you are that sort of a big game hunter.

CHAPTER TEN

Pressures, Primer Flattening and Case Expansion

While handloading his revolver ammunition, the average shooter has no elaborate pressure gun available to promptly advise him when he is running into dangerous pressures, and he probably would know nothing of its proper use if he did possess such intricate equipment. He is obliged to determine his pressures by more simple and practical, if far less accurate means. It has become the custom amongst shooters to observe the set-back and flattening of the primer in their fired cases and use this indication as a means of judging pressures. To my mind, this is a very uncertain manner of determination and this method should not be carried too far.

Primers, as made by the different ammunition companies and the Government arsenal, vary so much in thickness and composition of the metal cup, as well as in the power of their priming compositions, that they alone are no reliable indication of pressures. I have come to almost disregard primer flattening, as long as those primers are not pierced or do not protrude back into the firing pin hole in the recoil shield of the gun. However, with my most frequently used primer, the thick Remington nonmercuric, which is a very stout affair, I observe this flattening as one sign of pressure, but only to a limited extent. Other makes of primer are not so considered, owing to difference in construction: the new Winchester seems to be the thinnest of all; the Peters is about the same though, and even regular factory loads often show these primers flattened out and apparently flowing to the extreme edge of the cup, yet the pressures developed are only normal for the load. The primer may be badly flattened and yet the load be a normal one and entirely safe to use.

You can fire an empty case with primer alone, and the chances are that it will be flattened as badly as if a good load of powder were used, and it also will probably be driven back and partially out of the case. This is because all revolvers must have considerable headspace to insure rotation of the cylinder (and cases should be full length resized so they will fit rather loosely and freely in the chambers for this same reason). When you fire a loaded cartridge in a revolver, its primer starts to back out of the pocket, but the pressure of the load throws the head of the case back against the recoil shield, reseating the primer. (Colonel Hatcher has this very well illustrated in his big book). Fire this same case with primer alone in it and there is no set-back given the case which can reseat the protruding primer and it is therefore permitted to protrude and flatten out, possibly to a greater degree than if fired in the normally loaded cartridge.

In the cartridge case itself and its expansion we have the most reliable "practical" gauge to go by, outside the factory pressure gun. Whenever a fired revolver case extracts hard, then that powder charge, or combination of components, is altogether too powerful (possibly I should say "pressureful") for safety. The load should immediately be cut down at least a grain in weight and no more cartridges of that assembly should be fired. In double action, simultaneous ejection arms, the entire cylinder full of fired cases should at all times extract easily and freely, by a punch on the extractor rod from the palm of the hand. This is assuming of course that clean cases are used and they are not gummed or corroded in the chambers. If your cases expand to such an extent that it takes several blows and considerable effort to drive the extractor rod back and eject all six of those fired cases at once, then you are getting into heavy and dangerous pressures, and the load should be cut down or its components changed or modified. This may not call for a reduction in the powder charge, for that might not be the trouble at all. An oversized or too soft a bullet may be what is raising those pressures; but at any rate, whenever such signs of dangerous pressures are encountered, stop shooting that load *right then* and go over all its components until you have determined what *is* causing the trouble. Of course, good judgment dictates that the powder charge promptly be cut down a grain at least until the cause of the trouble has been determined. Nothing is to be gained by dangerous pressures; on the contrary, much is to be lost, including a good gun. Usually, velocities do not increase in proportion to the increase in pressures and with almost all powders, both rifle and revolver, after a certain "balance point" is reached in the load, any further increase to the charge is usually detrimental to accuracy and the slight additional velocity gained is not worth other sacrifices. One had better stick to what is known to be a safe combination and get the increased power from a new and improved powder when the manufacturers have released it and recommended it for higher velocities.

With the Colt Single Action, where the cases are ejected singly, any signs of tight cases should be heeded at once. In this gun, the bolt cuts, which stop the cylinder from revolving and align it for firing, are directly over the center of each chamber, and any undue pressure may bulge out these cuts and form a depression on the inside of the chamber into which case walls will expand. This will cause extraction troubles on all future loads, even light or normal charges. I have seen many of the older .45 Colt Single Action guns which had these bolt cuts bulged out from the firing of only heavy, black powder loads. At any rate, remember that the fired case is about your best safety gauge, watch extraction accordingly and be guided by it, with the flattening and other primer indications as a supplementary guide.

With well known primers which have been used considerably, you have a mental picture of just how they look after the different loads have been fired and one can often use these primers (and the old bean) as an additional indication of pressures developed. The indentation of the firing pin itself on the primer should always be watched. Any pierced primer, due to too much hammer-nose protrusion, extreme pressures, a rough, sharp or corroded firing pin, allows gas to be driven back into the works. This will in time cause corrosion of these parts; also minute particles of the copper cup will be blown back into the works and may jam the action. Very heavy pressures will also blow the firing pin indentation back into the firing pin hole and will thus tie up the gun so that it is very hard to revolve or open the cylinder of a double-action arm. Such things as these are always to be watched for and avoided at all costs. When the pressure raises to such an extent that it is too heavy for safe and certain results, it may cause leading or you may wake up, as I did once, and find only the grip, barrel and half the cylinder of your gun remaining in your hand and you will be lucky if some of the flying parts have not struck you, or worse still, hit some friend standing nearby. I spent a good many years finding out just what a sixgun would and would not stand, and as a result of experience, I now have a great deal more respect for some of the cautions and "Dont's" placed in the catalogs and handbooks on reloading.

There is one other indication of pressures, which, although a simple one, can be followed with a considerable amount of safe judgment. I refer to the sound of the cartridge upon being fired. Any experienced handloader or shooter can tell rather closely by the sound of his gun whether the load is a safe one or not. A certain caliber sounds quite distinctive upon being fired with standard cartridges. If the load is light it has a different report than a normal load, and if heavy still a different sound. When it begins to reach the dangerous stage, it has a still different, ear splitting, sharp crack. With a bit of practice one can accustom his ears to the sound of normal and safe reports, and the beginner should fire enough different makes of factory loads to become accustomed to the sound of what he knows to be safe, satisfactory ammunition for that caliber gun. The loads which are not heavy enough to fire cleanly, give off quite a hollow "punk" which can instantly be detected by the ear as being too light. In the same way, the old-timers could instantly tell when a muzzle loading, cap-and-ball rifle was properly loaded; if the charge was rammed down by some dub the report sounded quite prolonged and "spongy", while the same load put down the muzzle by an expert would crack like a blacksnake whip.

I do not claim that pressures may be judged by the report of the gun, but I do maintain that an experienced shooter can obtain a very close idea as to the safety of his loads by the sound of their report, and that beginners should train their ears to such indication. Also, in shooting a handgun, one should observe the indications of smoke given off when the cartridge is fired and should stop the moment any peculiarly colored or unduly large amount of smoke is seen. I was once shooting some factory loaded .38 Specials and fired a shot which gave off a most peculiar, reddish smoke from the rear end of the barrel. I stopped shooting, looked into the matter and discovered a bullet stuck half way up the bore. Any improperly burning powder charge gives off an excessive amount of smoke and will probably also fill the barrel and action with unburned powder grains. Watch out for such shots.

For most purposes a heavy revolver load is undesirable and not needed. Most practice shooting should be done with light or normal charges. There are times however, for game shooting, or defense purposes, or long range practice, when very powerful and extreme loads are needed, and for these purposes the hand loader should select the heaviest brass procurable, in new cases only. After being fired once with such loads, those cases should be used for normal or lighter charges. Heavy and magnum loads are exceedingly hard on cases and will soon split or crack them open after a few shots.

For all heavy or magnum loads select only the solid headed case, if possible to obtain such in the caliber cartridge you are using. I have illustrated the difference elsewhere in this book. If you *must* use your cases more than once for such loads, be sure they are full length resized before being reloaded. Remember that as brass is fired, worked and resized, it becomes more and more brittle and harder, and will crack in time—stop before that time arrives. New, unfired brass is somewhat elastic and can safely withstand the pressure of a single heavy load, whereas it might split with a second firing.

If the bore of your revolver becomes badly leaded from excessive pressures, or from too heavy a charge of too hot a powder which fuses the base of the bullets, it may then raise the pressures of all succeeding loads fired through it until that lead is removed. Accuracy will suffer also. A good, stiff brass bristle brush is about the best thing to remove this lead with. At times, you may encounter leading for no apparent reason, sometimes it is due to a rough or pitted barrel, or one with tight and loose places in it.

Throughout this book, I have constantly stressed the importance of some heavy loads being safe *only* in heavy .45 frame guns. Possibly, I had better state exactly what models of guns come under this classification, then there will be no mistake made by a beginner who might otherwise have a light framed gun blown up with a load which is only safe in a heavy framed model.

In Smith & Wesson make, the following models come under my classification of heavy frame guns: The Heavy Duty, encased ejector, 5″ police revolver in .38/44 caliber.

The Outdoorsman .38/44 caliber, with 6½″ barrel and target sights. The .44 caliber Military and Police models, which also take in the old Triple Lock S. & W. in .44 Special and other calibers. Lastly, the .357 S. & W. Magnum revolver. All these guns in their various calibers are built on heavy frames and are suitable for loads such as I have mentioned.

In Colt make, the Single Action and Bisley models come under the classification of heavy frame guns, but as I have previously mentioned, may not be suitable for the heaviest loads in the .45, .38/40 and .44/40 calibers. There is considerable difference in these however; the older guns which have the cylinder pin held in place by a set screw fitted through the front of the frame, are made of earlier materials than the later version which has a cross plate, base pin fastening, operated by spring tension. These later models, being made of better materials, are safer with heavier loads than are the older guns. The Colt New Service, in both plain and target models and the Shooting Master are all made on the .45 frame and are safe with heavy loads. The Colt Officer's Model is made on a .41 caliber frame and I do not consider it suitable or safe with the heavier .38 Special loads I have mentioned and listed.

Never attempt to reload any sort of cartridges for the cheaply made revolvers. Only Smith & Wesson or Colt guns should be used with reloaded ammunition. I remember one time a boy chum of mine obtained an old, nickle plated, break frame revolver for the .38 S. & W. cartridge, it was Iver Johnson or H. & R. make, and with it he got a box of old U. M. C. cartridges. We repaired to an old lime kiln near Helena, Montana to do a bit of shooting. Harold Garret decided that I, having had more experience than he, should do the shooting, so we proceeded along that line. I picked out a rock about the size of my hat and started shooting at it at a range of about twenty yards. My first shot went over the rock,

the second went low, so I then told Harold I would hit
it at the next shot. I did hit it too, but the top strap blew
off the gun at its junction with the ribbed barrel and went
whizzing back through my hat, parting my hair and giving
me a small scalp wound at the same time. The top of
one chamber was blown out and the barrel slowly flopped
over until it pointed at my feet. I looked at the gun, felt
my head and then chucked that bit of pot metal as far
down the gulch as I could. We found the piece of top
strap at the base of the old kiln, badly battered against
the rocks, so it must have had some velocity itself. From
that day on, neither one of us have ever monkeyed with
another such cheap handgun.

Never, under any circumstances, reload cartridges to be
used in one of these European imitations of our American
handguns. Some good handguns are made in Europe, but
they are not imitations of anything. I particularly refer to
the Spanish junk, advertised and stamped as "made for
the Smith & Wesson cartridge". These weapons are bad
enough when used with standard factory ammunition, many
of them split the barrel or blow out the top of a cylinder
even with it. So if you own one of these contraptions,
don't reload for it and don't try to trade it to some other
unsuspecting sucker—throw it away where it cannot be
recovered. Many of the handloads I recommend and use
safely in Smith & Wesson and Colt arms would blow these
imitations to pieces at the first shot, and although the
metal of their cylinders is too soft and weak to hold any
real sixgun pressures, it is plenty hard enough to cut a
hole in your skull if a piece strikes there when the gun
lets go.

It is well never to allow anyone to stand at one side of
a sixgun while it is being fired, especially with experimental loads. This applies with normal loads also, particularly if the cylinder is not fitted closely to the rear
end of the barrel and has excessive clearance here, or if
it is a gun which shaves the bullets in the least. Even

with the best of guns this is poor business, as the cylinder might not be locked in perfect alignment. Small particles of flying lead can strike a person in the face or eye with disastrous results. A bursting gun cylinder would be extremely dangerous to bystanders. With the old percussion guns this is particularly bad business, as fragments of the fired and bursting caps often fly out at right angles to the line of fire and many shooters have received bad eye injuries from this cause alone. Most of these old relics are badly rusted, or have been in that condition and restored, therefore extreme caution should be used when they are "tried out." They should always be shot held out at arm's length. Don't try any hip shooting, "throwing down" or other fool stunts, as the nipples may be badly rusted and permit considerable gas and cap fragments to fly outwards and up into the shooter's face if held close against the body. Such guns may easily put out one's eye.

CHAPTER ELEVEN

Working Up Special Loads

In working up special loads for any revolver or cartridge, always start with a charge which you *know* will be light and gradually increase its weight by not more than half a grain at a time, even when the case and primer show no signs whatever of pressure. Whenever the primer begins to flatten out and the case shows any expansion or signs of pressure, then it is best to make any further increase by about one-tenth of a grain at a time, stopping when a good, safe, satisfactory load is reached and always below the stage where the cases show the least signs of extracting hard, even when six are ejected simultaneously.

First, check the groove diameter of your gun if you do not already know it. Then check your bullet diameter, also note in what manner it may possibly differ from the standard bullet. If it has a deeper seating depth, cut the first charge very much lower than that recommended by the tables. I have stressed the importance of checking the seating depth of various bullets, also the difference in powder capacity with various bullets, also the difference in powder capacity of the various makes of case for the same cartridge. Remember always, that a deeper seating depth, other things being equal, will give higher pressures and a quicker and more complete combustion of the powder charge. A smaller powder chamber, due to thicker case walls, will do the same thing. A heavier crimp, whether due to cases longer than standard, or stretched and hardened by continued resizing, will also increase pressures. Too soft a bullet temper may also increase pressures, this being due to excessive upsettage in the cylinder throat or barrel cone. Remember that all hot powders, especially those like Bullseye, and #5 are not suitable for extreme or heavy loads, as they are much too fast and hot and may fuse the base of the bullet before they show signs of much pressure, leading the gun badly with consequent inaccurate results.

It is best to keep even heavy loads well within the limits of safety as shown by case expansion, and primer flattening to a lesser degree. Nothing is to be gained by going above the safety line with any load, as after that point is reached any increase in the powder charge seldom adds anything appreciable to velocity; on the contrary, it generally decreases the accuracy and even two-tenths of a grain increase may raise the pressures as much as three thousand pounds after the maximum safe figure is reached. It is well to stay within the safety margin, but by this I do not mean the 15,000 pounds pressure limit arbitrarily imposed by the loading companies for most revolver loads. This figure is necessitated by the fact that most, in fact, practically all, of the factory revolver cartridges loaded today *must* be safe if loaded into and fired from a revolver of their caliber made back in the '70s or '80s. The .357 Smith & Wesson Magnum is the first revolver cartridge developed since about 1908; think of that in this day when an automobile or radio three years old is an antique. What a bunch of saps we shooters are to swallow all this advertising patter about "modern" handguns.

With any of our lighter framed handguns, even with the .38 Military and Police and Official Police models in Smith & Wesson and Colt arms, it is safest to always stay around this 15,000 pounds limit. But with the thicker walled cylinder and barrels of the Smith & Wesson Heavy Duty Police revolver, the Outdoorsman and the .357 Magnum and with the Colt Single Action and New Service frame guns in the medium calibers, pressures can be raised to around double this limit. I know of some Heavy Duty

Smith & Wesson guns which I myself used for a long time, in which several hundred loads were fired developing up to 42,000 pounds pressure; also two Single Action Colts handled the same heavy charges of #80 powder for a similar long series of shots with no damage whatever. I am not recommending that such charges be duplicated or used; I am merely stating an actual occurrence. I have also used powder charges for years in my .44 Special Colt and Smith & Wesson guns which developed an average of 25,000 pounds pressure, with no trouble whatever from either hard extraction or damage to the guns. But such charges cannot be used as a steady diet in the .45 caliber cartridges, or in light frame .38 caliber arms, or in the .38/40 and .44/40 guns, as trouble is sure to develop sooner or later. Until the advent of the .357 Magnum, the .38 Colt Automatic cartridge was, if I remember right, our highest pressure handgun cartridge, its maximum running from 25,000 to 28,000 pounds—yet guns made back around 1908 are considered entirely safe at these figures.

For target shooting, nothing heavier than standard velocity is needed, certainly nothing over 900 feet with standard weight bullets. It is well to practice with such velocities, or even lighter loads. The latter will be far more pleasant to shoot and much more can be learned by their use. In the .38 Special, loads as light as 2½ to 3 grains of Bullseye with the standard weight bullet are plenty fast enough for twenty yard revolver work, whether in practice or serious competition. The longer fifty yard work usually requires more powerful charges, the standard velocity being about right at this range. In working up satisfactory light loads, trouble may be encountered to get the powder charge burning right; keep in mind that a heavy crimp can improve ignition, as can a heavier bullet, also seating the bullet deeper in the case. Bullseye is the best powder for really light and moderate loads, it takes an exceedingly fast powder which will burn at low pressures to do the trick. There may be occasions when it is necessary to seat a thick but light wad down on the powder charge to make it ignite and burn properly; this can only be done with the straight walled cases.

For hunting, the loads should be heavier than most standard cartridges. The bullets should by all means be of the flat point, sharp shoulder design or else with hollow points, even for small game shooting. If anything larger than small game is to be shot with the handgun, the shooter will need the most powerful handloads that his gun will safely handle with correctly shaped bullets—the most powerful combination he can shoot with accuracy.

Self defense work calls for the same ticket and most men of experience prefer heavy calibered guns for both hunting and defense, calibers such as the .357 Magnum, .38/40, .44/40, .44 Special and the various full loads in .45 caliber. Caliber has a great deal to do with actual killing power and the larger the hole you open in anything, the quicker you will kill it, other things such as penetration being equal. For this reason alone, if for no others, a properly loaded .44 Special will prove a more deadly killer than anything smaller; or larger either, with our present modeled guns. The smaller calibers will not cut such large holes and will not throw as much weight of lead. The present .45 guns are too thin in their cylinder walls to safely stand the pressures of the .44 Special heavy hand loads. And when it comes to using factory loads this is another and a much sadder story.

Some authorities claim that any revolver load which is heavier than the normal factory cartridge is not accurate. I cannot agree with this contention, as all of my best long range, game shooting has been accomplished with heavy loads in the .32/20, .38/44 Special, .357 Magnum and .44 Special arms. It is true that some men cannot shoot heavy loads with the same accuracy and effect that they can with the lighter and more pleasant charges, due to the heavier recoil and report of the former. In practice work or fine target competition, there is nothing to be gained and much to be lost by trying to hold down loads giving a heavy recoil and sharp muzzle blast, but in game or defense shooting, which never consists of firing a long string of shots, then these heavy loads are well worth while.

Some cartridges have a most ear splitting report when heavily loaded, the .32/20 being a particularly bad offender in this respect. Some shooters do not mind this at all, while with others it will in time develop a tendency to flinch and pull off the shots. The .357 Magnum cartridge gives quite a muzzle blast and report, especially when firing with the shorter barrels. Such noise, blast and recoil are absolutely unavoidable in shooting heavy loads, and one will simply have to become accustomed to them. Do not use such loads for your practice shooting, fire lighter charges in the gun for this, then you will not develop any bad habits. Under the excitement of defense work or in most game shooting, the report and recoil will never be noticed; in fact, the gun is apt to both feel and sound like a .22 caliber. I know this from experience. The few shots fired for such purposes will not interfere with anyone's nervous system to the extent of causing missing or flinching.

Many shooters will be desirous of working up a hand load which will shoot correctly with the fixed sights their gun is equipped with. At times, this becomes quite a problem. Usually a slow, heavy-bullet load will strike the target the highest of any, while very heavy, high velocity loads will generally strike lower—often low and left—so much so at times, that without adjustable sights it becomes quite a problem to hit with such loads. In most cases, this is due to the change in barrel time; the slow and heavy bullet has a much longer barrel time, hence the barrel raises higher in recoil before that bullet emerges from the muzzle. With a high velocity load in the same gun there is less barrel time and the bullet gets out of the barrel before it has raised so high from recoil. I took this matter up with Major Wesson some time ago, and he found that a higher rear sight was necessary for their .357 Magnum revolver when the standard .38 Special cartridge was used in the gun. Quite often, a lighter bullet at the same velocity will cause the gun to group to the left of its regular sighting.

The larger the caliber of the gun in proportion to its weight, the more uniform must be the shooter's grip on the gun butt to obtain equal accuracy and grouping on the target. Usually the very finest target accuracy will be obtained with normal to slightly over normal velocities. Some bullets shoot with uncanny accuracy at very high velocities, particularly those which were designed with this in mind. Others will not do so well if the standard velocity is increased.

By judicious examination and selection of the bullet weight and powder charge, it is often possible to have the gun with fixed sights shoot exactly to the point of aim. More often such guns will shoot too high, too low, or to one side or the other with the load the shooter particularly wishes to use. In general, the hand loader is best fitted with a target gun having adjustable sights, so that he may adjust it to shoot exactly right with his pet loads. Different revolver loads show just as much variation in their point of impact as do rifle loads, and adjustable sights are of equal importance if the shooter wants to hit anything. Anyone soon becomes plumb disgusted with a gun he cannot hit with.

In testing your handloads for accuracy, remember that quite often a load and bullet which shoots well and groups closely on the target at short range, may not carry well at all at long range. Really long range work with the revolver is the finest test of all for ammunition. I have seen ammunition used with considerable success in fast target competition which would have been hopeless for long range work. Long range work soon shows whether or not a bullet design is accurate. With too blunt a point it soon loses its accuracy. These true wad-cutter shapes lose out very fast after the fifty yard mark is passed, or if the wind is blowing whereas the longer pointed, better balanced bullets will retain their fine grouping qualities out to the extreme range.

In testing for shocking or killing power, remember that soap, wood and similar penetration or upsettage tests may mean very little. Bullets, even soft points from .32/20, .38/40 and .44/40 which may not expand in the least when fired into wood, merely smearing back the exposed lead tip, will nearly always expand perfectly on meat and bone. The real test of any such bullet is to kill game or live stock with it, then you find out darn quick just what it will and will not do. Living flesh, filled with blood, tissue and fluids acts differently on bullet metal, velocity and design; these soap and other substitute tests really mean very little in comparison.

If you want to catch your fired bullets in an undamaged condition to see how they are taking the rifling of the gun, one of the very best methods I know of is to shoot into soft snow drifts. Snow, unless packed very hard, will not expand or mark a bullet in the least, and the fired bullets may be recovered in the Spring or when the snow melts. I will admit that this may be a rather long drawn out test, but I have seen heavily loaded, hollow point bullets shot through a great deal of snow without deforming in the least, yet that same bullet would expand and turn wrong side out when shot through a jack rabbit. It is only by such hand loading and experimenting that we learn. Most of the few present improvements in revolver loads are directly due to the efforts of the individual experimenters.

I will close this chapter with a few of the heavy, maximum loads I have personally used. These cartridges are intended to be assembled by skilled and experienced shooters, from new, factory components, powder charges carefully weighed. Always start in with about two grains under the charge recommended and gradually work up. If the first one or two shots from a lot show signs of excessive pressure when fired, *Stop Right There* and either pull down or destroy the remainder of those loads. Then, starting with a lighter charge, again start working up, but be more gradual about it and check over all the components once more. Never be in a hurry when loading ammunition. *Make haste slowly* and good and safe results will be obtained—also ammunition that cannot be purchased over the counter.

.38/44 Special. Keith 160 grain hollow point, or hollow base bullet sized to .358″. Hercules #2400 powder. Charge 13.5 grains with either of the Ideal catalog numbers of this bullet: #358429 or #358431. With both bullets I have used as much as 8 grains by weight of duPont #80 the bullets being crimped in their crimp groove. Remington .38/44 cases and primers.

.357 Magnum Smith & Wesson. The two Keith bullets listed in preceding paragraph. Maximum charge 15 grains Hercules #2400, recommended charge 14.5 grains. Bullet diameter .358″.

.44 Smith & Wesson Special. Keith Lyman 250 grain flat base and 235 grain hollow point and hollow base. Ideal #429421 and #429422, used up to 20 grains of Hercules #2400, but this is a little too heavy. Recommended charge with the 235 grain bullet is 18.5 grains. The 250 grain Keith bullet can be used with 18 grains of this same powder. I have used up to 13.5 grains by weight #80 duPont with the hollow base and hollow point 235 grain bullet, and up to 13 grains of it with the 250 grain solid bullet.

.45 Colt, long case. Keith Lyman 250 grain flat base, and 235 grain hollow point Ideal #454424 bullets. I have used up to 22 grains of Hercules #2400 with bullets sized .452″ or .002″ over groove diameter in old guns running .450″ groove diameter and sized .454″ for newer guns with larger bore diameter. This charge can be used with all three bullets, but it is maximum. I have also used 15 grains by weight duPont #80.

.45 Auto Rim. In this cartridge I have used 9.5 grains of #80 in cases with solid heads and up to 10 grains, and in some cases, 11.5 grains, using very thin walled cases having the folding head or "semi balloon" primer pockets. Recommended charge for the 240 grain Keith-Lyman bullet #452423 is 9.5 grains of #80. The 235 grain Keith hollow point can be used with the same charge. Hercules Unique or duPont #5 are better powders for both the .45 Auto and this Auto Rim cases. Bullets sized .452".

BUT—remember Brother, I assume the risk and consequences of only such of the above loads as I myself assemble.

END